# PROTECTING OUR PLANET

# ENERGY EXTRACTION

BY REBECCA ROWELL

Essential Library
An Imprint of Abdo Publishing
abdobooks.com

**ABDOBOOKS.COM**

Published by Abdo Publishing, a division of ABDO, PO Box 398166, Minneapolis, Minnesota 55439. Copyright © 2025 by Abdo Consulting Group, Inc. International copyrights reserved in all countries. No part of this book may be reproduced in any form without written permission from the publisher. Essential Library™ is a trademark and logo of Abdo Publishing.

Printed in the United States of America, North Mankato, Minnesota.

052024
092024

THIS BOOK CONTAINS RECYCLED MATERIALS

Cover Photo: Shutterstock Images
Interior Photos: David McNew/Getty Images News/Getty Images, 4, 7; Brian van der Brug/Los Angeles Times/Getty Images, 8–9; Bruce Cox/Los Angeles Times/Getty Images, 12–13; Shawn Goldberg/Shutterstock Images, 17; Monkey Business Images/Shutterstock Images, 18; Shutterstock Images, 23, 48, 52, 63, 91, 100; Jouni Niskakoski/Shutterstock Images, 24–25; Maya Siddiqui/Bloomberg/Getty Images, 26; Universal History Archive/Universal Images Group/Getty Images, 28, 31; Bettmann/Getty Images, 34; Ty Wright/Bloomberg/Getty Images, 38; Alexander Manzyuk/Anadolu Agency/Getty Images, 41; Mario Tama/Getty Images News/Getty Images, 42; Umit Turhan Coskun/NurPhoto/Getty Images, 45; Andrey Rudakov/Bloomberg/Getty Images, 51; Mindy Schauer/MediaNews Group/Orange County Register/Getty Images, 56; Virginie Clavieres/Paris Match Archive/Getty Images, 59; Scott Dalton/Bloomberg/Getty Images, 60; David Paul Morris/Bloomberg/Getty Images, 66–67; Ben Garver/The Berkshire Eagle/AP Images, 68; Daniel Acker/Bloomberg/Getty Images, 71; Rachel Woolf/Bloomberg/Getty Images, 72; Paul Ratje/AFP/Getty Images, 76; J. Pat Carter/Getty Images Sport/Getty Images, 78–79; Sarah Silbiger/Getty Images News/Getty Images, 83; Helen H. Richardson/Denver Post/Getty Images, 84–85; Christie Cooper/Shutterstock Images, 86; Chang Lee/Shutterstock Images, 88–89; Tara Ziemba/WireImage/Getty Images, 94; William Campbell/Getty Images News/Getty Images, 97; Wang Dongzhen/Xinhua News Agency/Getty Images, 98; Jeff Whyte/Shutterstock Images, 101

Editor: Arnold Ringstad and Haley Williams
Series Designer: Cynthia Della-Rovere

Library of Congress Control Number: 2023949404

**PUBLISHER'S CATALOGING-IN-PUBLICATION DATA**
Names: Rowell, Rebecca, author.
Title: Energy extraction / by Rebecca Rowell
Description: Minneapolis, Minnesota: Abdo Publishing, 2025 | Series: Protecting our planet | Includes online resources and index.
Identifiers: ISBN 9781098293437 (lib. bdg.) | ISBN 9798384912705 (ebook)
Subjects: LCSH: Fossil fuels--Juvenile literature. | Geothermal engineering--Juvenile literature. | Solar energy--Juvenile literature. | Ocean wave power--Juvenile literature. | Wind power--Juvenile literature. | Energy consumption--Forecasting--Juvenile literature.
Classification: DDC 333.951--dc23

# CONTENTS

**CHAPTER 1**
THE OILY BEACH................................................................ 4

**CHAPTER 2**
THE SCIENCE OF FOSSIL FUELS.......................................18

**CHAPTER 3**
THE HISTORY OF ENERGY EXTRACTION........................28

**CHAPTER 4**
EXTRACTING COAL...........................................................38

**CHAPTER 5**
EXTRACTING OIL..............................................................48

**CHAPTER 6**
EXTRACTING NATURAL GAS ...........................................60

**CHAPTER 7**
FRACKING.........................................................................72

**CHAPTER 8**
GET INVOLVED IN SOLUTIONS........................................86

ESSENTIAL FACTS ............................................ 100
GLOSSARY ........................................................ 102
ADDITIONAL RESOURCES................................. 104
SOURCE NOTES................................................ 106
INDEX ............................................................... 110
ABOUT THE AUTHOR ........................................ 112

A 2015 oil spill at Refugio State Beach in California spread across about four miles (6.4 km) of the popular beach.

# CHAPTER 1

# THE OILY BEACH

It was May 19, 2015, and Ethan was home and enjoying an unexpected day off from school. A burst water pipe in the school had resulted in canceled classes. Ethan slept a couple extra hours, then enjoyed a heaping bowl of his favorite cereal for breakfast. Next, he played video games during what would normally be his English class.

It was midmorning, and Ethan flipped on the television for some company. He scrolled through his social media feeds. Ethan was looking forward to seeing what his friends were doing on their free day. But the television grabbed his attention instead.

A local news station was reporting a story at Refugio State Beach. The California beach was not far from his home in Santa Barbara. Ethan and his friends enjoyed relaxing at the beach and hiking along its trails. Just last week, they had a group picnic there and played Frisbee in the sand.

Ethan did not need to see the shot of the Refugio State Beach sign to know the locale. He recognized it immediately, but the beach on his television screen looked dramatically different from

## Oil Pipelines

Oil pipelines move oil from the sites where it is extracted from the ground to facilities called refineries, where it is turned into usable products such as gasoline and kerosene. Operating around the clock, pipelines provide an efficient way to transport oil long distances. Most of the time they are safe, but spills can become high-profile events with severe environmental consequences. More than 190,000 miles (306,000 km) of oil pipelines crisscross the United States.[3]

the beach he frequented and loved. Black oil covered a swath of the coast. The beautiful blue waters were dark, and the shoreline rocks were stained.

He was not sure, but Ethan thought he saw beached fish coated in the oil that blanketed the surf and beach. It all looked so wrong. Something terrible had happened there.

Ethan put his phone down and focused on the news report. The anchor explained that an oil pipeline ruptured earlier that day. The pipeline ran just north of US Highway 101, a road that followed the coastline. Known as Line 901, the pipeline was 24 inches (61 cm) in diameter and carried about 50,400 gallons (190,800 L) of oil per hour.[1] Officials estimated that more than 100,000 gallons (379,000 L) spilled in the few hours before crews could stop the leak.[2]

The oil had run down a storm drain, flowed into a ravine beneath the highway, and spilled into the ocean. Behind the reporter on the scene, people appeared to be cleaning up the beach. Seeing that, Ethan shut off the TV, put on his shoes, hopped on his bike, and headed to the beach to join them.

This seemed like a better use of his day off than playing video games and spending time on social media.

## ON THE BEACH

When Ethan reached the beach, he saw a lot of people working hard to clean up the mess. Some were using rakes to separate the oil from the sand and collect it into piles. Others were scooping up oil with shovels and putting it in buckets to be carried off the beach. A few even had gloves on so they could use their hands to remove the oil from the ground.

Lobsters were among the many species affected by the Refugio oil spill.

Everything seemed messy, including people's clothing, which was stained with oil. Even the overall recovery effort looked disorganized, as if there wasn't anyone in charge. Some local police officers were watching the scene, but Ethan saw no evidence of an official cleanup.

Ethan stopped the first volunteer he encountered, a mother who was picking up oil alongside her teenage daughter. The volunteer explained that she cared deeply about the environment and, like Ethan, had come to the beach as soon as she heard about the spill. She took her daughter out of school

Residents in nearby Santa Barbara took it upon themselves to collect oil and clean up their beach despite warnings from officials.

for the day to rescue wildlife at the oil-covered beach. When they could not find living creatures to save, they decided to start picking up oil.

The volunteer was surprised to see no one running an official cleanup operation. Along with a few other people who arrived, the mother and daughter team started doing whatever they could. A local home improvement store had donated buckets, and the volunteers were gathering up as much oil as possible.

The volunteer explained that police had asked her and the other volunteers to leave. The officers said the oil was hazardous and that experts would arrive to direct the cleanup. But those experts were nowhere to be found. Knowing the importance of cleaning up the oil as quickly as possible, several volunteers had decided to ignore the authorities and continue removing oil. The volunteers could not stand to see their beloved beach in this condition.

More authorities arrived soon, and the group of volunteers began to thin. Ethan was eager to help, but he also did not want to get sick. During his short time at the beach, the oil fumes were already starting to make him feel a little ill. He headed home, determined to continue following the story closely.

# FOLLOWING THE STORY

Ethan followed the developments in the Refugio State Beach oil spill online, on television, and in the local newspaper. Within a few days, he saw that authorities created an online registration program to let volunteers get involved in a safe, effective, and organized way. Soon, crews of trained volunteers, equipped with personal protective gear, were helping clean the beach. Experts were overseeing safety at the oil spill site. Approximately 300 volunteers were trained, with more than half of them focusing on cleaning oil at the beach.[4]

At the same time, a large-scale professional cleanup effort began. More than 1,100 people were involved, and they helped in the air, on the ground, and on the water. Some piloted two helicopters, assessing the damage from above. Others operated three specialized tanker trucks equipped with vacuums to suck up oil on the ground. More professionals crewed 21 boats that skimmed the water along the shore to collect oil sitting on the surface.[5]

The scope of the spill's damage became clear during the response. Local authorities shut down nearby fisheries and closed recreational beaches. The spill happened just before Memorial Day, so it had a significant financial impact by canceling holiday weekend beach outings.

The spill harmed or killed many fish, invertebrates, birds, and marine mammals in the affected area. This included species such as the brown pelican, California sea lion, and surf perch. Authorities collected 202 dead birds and 99 dead marine mammals.[6]

# ECHOES OF THE PAST

Ethan was impressed with the spirit of the early volunteers, and he was glad the authorities found a way to safely clean up the

> **Cultural Impact**
> Environmental disasters such as oil spills can harm more than plants, animals, and ecosystems. They can also affect an area's cultural heritage. Soon after the Refugio State Beach oil spill began, authorities recognized that the pollution and the response efforts could affect American Indian cultural and historical sites nearby. When planning the cleanup response, authorities trained cultural monitors and archaeologists to accompany the cleanup crews to oversee their work and ensure any important sites were protected.

beach he loved. Still, he felt frustrated and sad that the spill caused all this work. He spoke with his grandmother about how he wished more could be done.

What Ethan's grandmother said surprised him. She had also seen firsthand the effects of an oil spill in Santa Barbara.

Protesters gathered to block access to a Santa Barbara wharf on the first anniversary of the 1969 spill.

It was in January of 1969. A drilling platform only six miles (9.7 km) off the coast caused a spill after the company operating it took shortcuts with safety measures. Oil poured into the water. The spill continued for days before workers could finally stop the flow. About three million gallons (11.4 million L)

entered the water, making it the largest oil spill in US history at the time.⁷

Ethan's grandmother described seeing the local beaches covered in oil. The sticky, suffocating material killed thousands of birds on the shoreline. She said she loved visiting the beaches and felt sad and angry to see them in this state. Hearing her story reminded Ethan of how he felt when he arrived at Refugio State Beach after the pipeline spill.

Like Ethan, his grandmother had searched for solutions after the disaster. She was not alone. Activists pushed for new rules about oil drilling. They advocated for tougher laws to protect the environment.

The spill captured the attention of the nation, and politicians got involved. Ethan's grandmother had watched as President Richard Nixon visited one of the affected beaches in the aftermath of the spill. She still remembered what he said: "The Santa Barbara incident has frankly touched the conscience

> **Earth Day**
> One of the politicians who visited the site of the 1969 Santa Barbara oil spill was Wisconsin senator Gaylord Nelson. He was known for his environmentalist views. The visit, along with the widespread activism of the 1960s, helped inspire him to create a day for education about the environment. He said, "I am convinced that the same concern the youth of this nation took in changing this nation's priorities on the war in Vietnam and on civil rights can be shown for the problems of the environment."⁸ This day of education, first held on April 22, 1970, later became known as Earth Day. It remains an annual event focused on protecting the environment.

of the American people."⁹ The next year, he created the Environmental Protection Agency (EPA), which helps prevent and respond to environmental crises. The 1969 spill helped inspire a new wave of the environmental movement.

# INSPIRED TO ACT

Ethan was inspired, too. He decided he wanted to take action. He spoke at city council meetings and wrote letters to the newspaper about making sure the community was prepared for oil cleanups and similar environmental disasters.

Ethan wrote to California government officials in charge of regulating oil pipelines, encouraging them to improve safety. And he wrote to his representatives in US Congress about policies for reducing the use of oil in the first place. He suggested replacing oil with energy sources that carry less risk of polluting the environment.

Ethan's experience at Refugio State Beach also influenced his studies. He decided that he was going to study environmental science in college to learn more about the world's vulnerable ecosystems, how to protect them, and how to help them

> **We are pleased to join this agreement with industry and our co-trustees to help restore vital habitats, wildlife, and recreational areas injured by this oil spill. Local communities and economies depend on these ecosystems.**[10]
>
> —Nicole LeBoeuf, National Ocean Service, on the Refugio Beach Oil Spill settlement, 2020

recover from disasters. He was also going to continue following the developments in the story of Refugio State Beach.

Five years after the spill, the US Department of Justice finalized a settlement with the oil pipeline company responsible for the disaster. An investigation showed that the company did not properly maintain its pipeline, failing to fix corrosion that developed over time. As part of the settlement, the company had to improve maintenance standards for its pipelines throughout the United States. It also had to pay $22.3 million to restore local habitats.[11]

Ethan was glad to hear the company had been held accountable. He thought it was important for those responsible for the spill to take part in restoration efforts. Thinking back on that day off from school when he saw the effects of an oil spill firsthand, he felt more determined than ever to protect the environment from similar disasters in the future.

People who speak out against issues affecting their community can help bring attention to those issues.

In the United States, about 45 percent of oil is used to make gasoline.

CHAPTER 2

# THE SCIENCE OF FOSSIL FUELS

Every day, people rely on energy from fossil fuels such as oil, coal, and natural gas. In 2020, these fuels provided 80 percent of the energy on the planet.[1] Gasoline, which is created from oil, powers cars, motorcycles, and buses. Electricity from coal-fired plants lights up buildings, brings computers to life, and keeps air conditioners running on hot days. Natural gas fuels stoves and provides heat and hot water for homes.

Fossil fuels are often found deep underground, and it can take great effort and considerable amounts of money to access them. Energy extraction is the process of drilling or mining to bring fossil fuels to the surface. Once the fossil fuels have been extracted, they can then be processed and transported for use. Vast amounts of these fuels are used for energy, and this supply will not last forever.

Fossil fuels are nonrenewable resources. This means that the natural processes that create them cannot keep up with the speed at which people use them. The planet has a finite amount of fossil fuels.

# TYPES AND ORIGINS

Fossil fuels developed from the fossilized remains of animals and plants that lived millions of years ago. Not all fossil fuels had the same start. Oil and natural gas come from the remains of animals. These fuels were once plankton, microscopic life forms that were abundant in warm oceans.

When these plankton died, they sank to the ocean floor. The oxygen-free environment there kept bacteria, which need oxygen, away. They were unable to eat the dead plankton. Instead, layers of sediment covered the plankton over many years, burying them deeper and deeper in the earth.

Coal started as plants. Approximately 300 million years ago, Earth had masses of swamp forests, areas covered in warm water in which plants such as tree ferns grew and thrived. When the plants died, they fell into the water. But they did not decay. As with the plankton, a lack of oxygen in the

## Fossil Fuel Subsidies

Governments worldwide provide subsidies to support the fossil fuel industry financially. Some subsidies are grants to energy companies. Others include loans with low interest rates or land priced lower than it would be for other buyers. The International Monetary Fund (IMF), a financial agency of the United Nations, tracks this spending. The subsidies total trillions of dollars, and the amounts have been growing, increasing from $5 trillion in 2020 to $5.9 trillion in 2021 and $7 trillion in 2022. Critics argue that subsidies provide an incentive to use more fossil fuels. The IMF notes, "Scaling back subsidies would reduce air pollution, generate revenue, and make a major contribution to slowing climate change."[2]

water kept bacteria away. The plants became buried, ending up deep underground.

As the dead plankton and plants moved farther underground, the material faced increased heat and pressure. These factors caused the fossils to break down and start the process of becoming fossil fuels. After thousands of years, plankton became kerogen and plants became peat. Kerogen and peat are fuels, but they are not fossil fuels. They do not carry as much energy as oil, natural gas, or coal. Eventually, after being subjected to heat and pressure underground for millions of years, the substances in plankton become oil and natural gas, and the substances in plants become coal.

**It takes about ten feet (3 m) of plant material to eventually create one foot (0.3 m) of coal.[3]**

Oil can vary in appearance. While it is often black or dark brown, it can also have a reddish, greenish, or yellowish hue. It can even appear almost clear. This variability is due to the chemical makeup of the particular oil. For example, oil that is almost clear contains little sulfur and few metals. Coal looks like rock. Like oil, it is usually black or dark brown. Unlike coal and oil, natural gas is not a solid or liquid and cannot be seen.

# HOW THEY ARE USED

The energy stored in fossil fuels is what makes them so appealing to humans. This energy comes primarily from the carbon and hydrogen that existed in the plankton and plants when they were alive. Burning oil, natural gas, and coal releases that energy, providing the power that runs machinery and technology.

Humans also rely on these substances for nonfuel uses. Petrochemicals are chemicals made from natural gas and oil. Products involving petrochemicals are part of daily life. They include detergents, drugs, flooring, insulation, paints, plastics, and synthetic fibers. Petrochemicals are used to make a wide range of products, such as airplane parts, aspirin, compact discs, polyester clothing, and suitcases.

## The Importance of Peat

Peat, also known as peat moss and sphagnum moss, plays an important role in fighting climate change. It traps carbon from the atmosphere, helping counteract global warming. Peatlands, or bogs, have been harvested for use in agriculture. Soil companies add peat to their mixes to help the dirt hold moisture and to support drainage. These are good things for growing healthy plants, but harvesting peat decreases the amount of carbon that bogs can store. Peat develops slowly, only a few feet in thousands of years. In an effort to help peat bogs, the United Kingdom banned the commercial sale of peat starting in 2024.

# HOW THEY ARE LOCATED

Oil, coal, and natural gas are usually deep underground, from a few hundred feet to a couple miles below the surface. They are often surrounded by thick layers of rock. Energy companies rely on geologists to find spots where fossil fuels may be located. These scientists study layers of rock to locate stores of oil, natural gas, or coal.

Coal is classified into different types based on its carbon content.

One method to find fossil fuels is a seismic survey, a test in which geologists create a vibration in the ground to find oil or natural gas. On land, the vibration might come from a special vibrating pad or a small explosive. Seismic surveys in the ocean use sound waves to understand the rock below the ocean's floor. Studying the echoes from these tests can tell geologists a lot about what lies underground.

When conducting seismic surveys, geologists are looking for sedimentary rock formations. Sedimentary rocks are porous, meaning they are full of small spaces. These spaces may contain

Enormous seismic survey vessels deploy a variety of equipment to detect undersea fossil fuel reserves.

oil and natural gas. Oil is usually found in limestone or sandstone. Natural gas is often found in shale. When geologists suspect an area has oil or natural gas, they can carry out exploratory drilling to confirm the findings.

Geologists use multiple processes to locate coal. They create detailed geological maps of an area to help find places where coal is likely to be, accounting for known coal locations, the rock layers in an area, and the types of rock involved.

Aerial photographs can give geologists a better understanding of the landscape during these searches. Finally, exploratory drilling confirms the existence of coal and allows geologists to gather samples to plan later mining activity.

## WHERE THEY ARE

Fossil fuels have been found around the world, both beneath land and water. The regions and environments these fuels are found in vary dramatically. Almost half of known oil reserves are in the Middle East.[4] Latin America and North America also have significant reserves, as do other regions. Venezuela had the largest oil reserves of any country in 2021, mostly located offshore. Because oil comes from long-dead sea life, the presence of oil indicates that an area was once covered by oceans. This includes the Middle East, which is mostly desert and is extremely hot and dry.

Saudi Arabia is among several Middle Eastern countries with extensive oil drilling and refining infrastructure. The nation produced more than 12 million barrels of oil per day in 2022.

Because oil and natural gas develop from the same source, natural gas has been found in the same places as oil. Countries with major oil reserves also have large natural gas reserves. Russia and the United States are the nations with the most natural gas reserves. As with oil, the presence of natural gas reveals what the landscape was like during prehistoric times. These regions were once covered by seawater rich in plankton.

Coal is also distributed widely around the world. However, much of it is concentrated in a few countries. The United States, home to 23 percent of global coal reserves, has the largest share. Behind it are Russia at 15 percent, Australia at 14 percent, and China at 13 percent.[5] The existence of coal reserves indicates the land was swampy and packed with vegetation millions of years ago.

## Resources, Reserves, and Production

Scientists and others measure fossil fuels in different ways, including in terms of resources, reserves, and production. Resources are estimates of the total amounts of fuels underground. Reserves are known amounts of fossil fuels that can be removed and processed into a usable form. Production is the amount of a fossil fuel extracted and processed in a particular span of time, such as a year.

Chopped wood was once a key source of energy in daily life, but this changed as people learned how to extract and use fossil fuels.

CHAPTER 3

# THE HISTORY OF ENERGY EXTRACTION

Humans have been using fossil fuels for thousands of years. Over the centuries, as civilizations advanced and discovered new sources of energy, energy consumption changed. Fossil fuels became the dominant energy sources for the world.

In the United States, the main source of energy moved from wood in the 1700s to fossil fuels in the 1800s. This occurred because people figured out how to find, access, process, and transport fossil fuels. In the 1900s and 2000s, mining and drilling methods developed, increasing the amounts of fossil fuels people could extract. At the same time, the public became more aware of the environmental issues energy extraction can cause.

## ANCIENT FOSSIL FUELS

Long before fossil fuels powered cars and power plants, ancient people discovered these substances near Earth's surface and found ways to use them. Archaeologists believe people in what is now Wales used coal to help funeral pyres burn. In China around the 200s BCE, people burned coal for heat and used the material

### What Is Oil?

The term *oil* refers to greasy liquids that do not mix with water. It includes substances with a variety of different makeups and uses. The fossil fuel commonly called *oil* is made of hydrocarbons and is also known as crude oil or petroleum. Other types of naturally occurring oil, such as oil from the bodies of whales, have also been used as fuel sources in the past. Cooking oils, such as vegetable oil, are made from fatty acids and add nutrition and flavor to food.

in trading. As early as the 1100s CE, the Hopi people in what is now the southwest United States burned coal for cooking and heat. In the following centuries, they began using heat from coal in the production of pottery.

Like coal, oil has been used for thousands of years. In ancient Egypt, oil had medicinal uses. People used it to care for wounds and as a laxative. Assyrians, ancient people in areas of what is now the Middle East, used oil in a very different way by heating and then pouring it over the heads of criminals as a form of punishment. The ancient Chinese burned oil to generate heat and to evaporate salt water to produce salt.

Natural gas was found and used by ancient people, too. Gas seeping from underground in what is now Azerbaijan may have been ignited by lightning, creating a flame that inspired a fire cult in ancient times. The Chinese burned natural gas to boil ocean water to make it drinkable.

## EARLY HISTORY OF COAL MINING

The first known extraction of coal took place in China approximately 3,000 years ago, though the mining method is unknown. The Romans discovered coal in Great Britain after invading the island in 43 CE, but are not known to have set up significant mining operations for it. Evidence of coal use in Britain has been found at sites along the wall the ancient Romans built, particularly near Northumberland, where outcrops of coal exist. These seams of coal are at or near the surface, making it easy to access the coal without mining.

The first major shipment of coal to reach London, England, arrived in 1228. It was delivered from Northumberland and from Fife, Scotland. But it was not mined. Rather, outcrops of coal in these regions were in the North Sea, below water. The moving water broke off pieces of coal that then washed ashore, where women and children collected them.

Most early coal collection occurred in places where outcrops were exposed and easily accessible. Once these sources were

Coal mining has long been challenging, dangerous work.

used up, people had to go below ground for coal. Early shaft, or underground, mines were essentially like water wells, narrow holes dug deep into the ground. Tunnels known as adits branched off to allow water to drain from the shafts.

Once the coal was exhausted, miners extended shafts deeper into the ground and expanded the bottom of the shafts. In the 1300s, the increasing use of coal led to the depletion of some shallower mines. The coal mining industry grew.

Digging deeper shafts required new methods for moving water out of the shaft. Workers filled buckets with water and put them on chains to be pulled to the surface. Initially, people provided the pulling power, but horses later took over. Water removal systems developed over time. Eventually, people used windmills to pump water out of the ground through pipes. Until the early 1700s, the challenges of water removal limited the depth of a coal shaft to about 350 feet (105 m).[1]

**In 1684, the city of Bristol, England, was surrounded by 70 mines, and coal mining employed only 123 people.[2]**

Early mining involved chipping coal with a pick. Miners later began using dynamite to blow coal out of a seam. Mining changed dramatically in 1868 with the invention of a cutting machine powered by steam. In 1891, the longwall cutter was invented. It allowed for continuous cutting down the length of a seam.

For many decades, the coal mining process was to cut, drill, blast, and load, with one step being performed at a time. In the

1940s, machines known as continuous miners could do more than one of these steps at a time. This included removing coal from the earth and then hauling it to equipment that would transport it to the surface.

In the 1960s, mountaintop removal mining began in the United States. Blowing off the tops of mountains with explosives provided easy access to the coal within. The method was effective, but many people were upset about its environmental effects. In the early 2000s, some activists protested mountaintop mining by standing in the way of mines to prevent workers from entering and by chaining themselves to mining equipment.

## Coal Mining in Missouri

The history of coal mining in Missouri demonstrates the change in people's thinking about the environmental effects of coal extraction over time. People began mining for coal in Missouri in the 1840s. For more than a century, coal mining continued with almost no regulations. This damaged thousands of acres of forests and farmland. Acid drained from mining operations, sediments flowed into streams, and soil eroded. The state eventually began regulating mining, passing laws in the 1970s and 1980s that put rules and restrictions in place. The laws required coal companies to assess the geology, wildlife, and cultural resources of proposed mining areas. These companies had to replace the fertile agricultural soil that was displaced by the mining process.

# EARLY HISTORY OF OIL EXTRACTION

The first oil well on record was drilled in 350 CE by the Chinese. They used bamboo for drilling and as pipelines. Wells were as deep as 800 feet (244 m).[3] Over the centuries, different cultures

Edwin L. Drake, *front right*, was a pioneer in oil extraction but never became wealthy from his work.

discovered new uses for oil. The fuel was energy-rich and easier to transport than fuels such as coal or wood. But extracting oil from underground was challenging.

In 1859, businessman Edwin L. Drake constructed an oil well in northwestern Pennsylvania. It was the first well designed specifically to pump oil, and it was a key moment in the modern oil industry. Soon after, many more oil wells were built across the United States and around the world.

Refineries were also built to transform oil into usable fuels, such as kerosene. The invention of the internal combustion engine and the rise of cars for transportation in the early 1900s dramatically increased the demand for oil. Nations with oil reserves became rich by extracting and selling the substance.

Oil production carries significant risks, though. Sometimes, an incident can cause oil to spill while being extracted or transported, resulting in severe environmental damage. These risks became widely known to Americans with the 1969 Santa Barbara oil spill, which remains one of the worst oil spills in US history.

In 1989, the oil tanker *Exxon Valdez* got stuck in shallow water off the coast of Alaska. The tanker spilled millions of gallons of oil along a vast portion of the Alaskan coast. The spill also killed a lot of wildlife. In 2010, the *Deepwater Horizon* oil rig in the Gulf of Mexico exploded and sank. The explosion killed 11 workers and caused oil to spill into the sea. From when the explosion occurred in April to when the well was finally sealed in September, the rig released millions of gallons of oil, polluting more than 1,000 miles (1,600 km) of shoreline along the gulf.[4]

## EARLY HISTORY OF NATURAL GAS EXTRACTION

As they had done with oil, the Chinese used bamboo as pipelines to carry natural gas. Many centuries later, natural gas became a commodity in England in 1785, where it was used to fuel lamps. Three decades later in 1816, Baltimore, Maryland, became the first US city to fuel streetlamps with natural gas. Then in 1821, Fredonia, New York, became the site of the first natural gas well in the United States. The company behind the well piped the gas throughout the town for lighting purposes.

Early pipeline technology limited the use of natural gas to local areas. Pipelines at the time simply could not transport natural gas long distances. But advances in pipelines in the 1890s allowed people to transport natural gas up to approximately 100 miles (160 km).[5]

The 1920s brought even more development, allowing the construction of pipeline

> " In 2010, we promised to help the Gulf of Mexico recover, become a safer, better company, and report on our progress. The lessons we've learned and the changes we've made—from tougher standards to better oversight—are at the core of becoming a safer company.[6] "
>
> —Statement from BP, the company responsible for the Deepwater Horizon disaster, 2020

networks over even greater distances. The more widespread use of natural gas also highlighted the dangers of extracting and transporting the substance. Accumulated natural gas can trigger an explosion when exposed to a spark, which can destroy infrastructure and injure or kill people and animals. High-profile disasters in the early 1900s led to stronger safety regulations around the use of natural gas.

Over the centuries, humans have come to realize many benefits from fossil fuels. These substances have provided the energy to light and heat homes and businesses. They powered the vehicles and machinery that built the modern world. As these fuels have increased in importance, scientists and inventors have found new ways to locate, access, extract, and use coal, oil, and natural gas. At the same time, experts and the general public have also begun to see the negative effects the fossil fuel industry can have on people and the environment.

### The Risks of Natural Gas

The risks of extracting and using natural gas became clear in a 1937 incident. New London, Texas, had a wealth of oil and natural gas reserves, and the local school was near an extraction site. School officials decided to tap into a line containing residue gas, a processed form of natural gas, to save money on energy costs. But a leak caused the colorless, odorless gas to accumulate under the school. On March 18, a spark caused an explosion that destroyed the entire school, killing about 300 people.[7] The disaster led to new rules for adding odor-creating substances to natural gas, giving people a chance to detect future leaks before it is too late.

Conveyor belts in mines help carry coal up to the surface.

## CHAPTER 4

# EXTRACTING COAL

Modern coal mining is done underground or at the surface. Underground mining has four methods. They are room-and-pillar, longwall, shortwall, and thick-seam. Room-and-pillar mining is the most common type of underground mining. It is used to mine coal fields that are mostly flat. This method creates a grid in the coal bed, cutting out rooms in the coal while leaving pillars to support the rock above.

Room-and-pillar mining is done in two ways. In the conventional method, different machines and teams of miners perform the mining tasks of undercutting, drilling, blasting, and loading. In the continuous mining method, a piece of equipment called a continuous miner tears coal from the earth and puts it into a vehicle for transport. Once coal is removed from a seam, it is moved from the mine to the surface. The act of transporting coal from below ground is known as coal haulage.

In longwall mining, machines process and extract enormous blocks of coal along a broad underground wall. Shortwall mining is similar but involves a narrower wall of coal. Thick-seam

> ## Cleaning Coal
> The main goal of cleaning coal during processing is to remove impurities. Any other rocks or substances in the coal reduce how much heat can be produced when the coal is burned. Cleaning also helps reduce air pollution. When ash, rocks, and sulfur are burned with the coal, they release harmful material into the atmosphere. Pollution laws require coal to be cleaned of these harmful substances.

mining is used when the underground seam of coal is unusually broad. The seam is broken up into slices that are processed separately.

Surface mining is used when the coal seam is less than 200 feet (61 m) underground.[1] The process involves clearing the land and removing and storing the topsoil, which is replaced later on. Next, the hard layer above the coal seam is drilled, blown into pieces with explosives, and cleared off to expose the coal seam. The coal seam is then cleaned. After that, the seam is broken up by drilling and using explosives. The resulting coal pieces are conveyed out of the mine and then transported to a processing facility.

An extreme form of surface mining is mountaintop removal. As the name suggests, this type of mining involves removing the tops of mountains. Explosives blast away hundreds of feet of the mountain to expose the coal within. In the United States, mountaintop removal is common in the Appalachian Mountains. The method has been used in several states, with most of it occurring in eastern Kentucky, southwestern Virginia, southern West Virginia, and eastern Tennessee.

# PROCESSING AND TRANSPORTING

Once coal is removed from the ground, it must be processed for use. Coal extracted from a mine may include other substances, such as clay and rock, that need to be removed. In addition, material from the roof or floor of the mine may be carried away with the coal. During processing, coal is cleaned and crushed into smaller sizes.

After processing, coal can be transported. Trains are the most common method for moving coal long distances. Trucks can be used for shorter distances and for smaller loads of less than 25 short tons (22.7 metric tons). Some coal is transported via water using barges. In the United States, barges carry coal

Mining at the surface often involves large pieces of equipment, such as bucket-wheel excavators.

Mountaintop removal destroys habitats and has long-lasting effects on the surrounding ecosystems.

on the Mississippi River as well as the Cumberland, Ohio, and Tennessee Rivers. Barges on these rivers can carry as much as 1,500 short tons (1,360 metric tons).[2]

Pipelines are another method for transporting coal. They move a slurry that is a mixture of coal and a liquid, such as water, oil, or methanol. In Europe and the United States, coal slurry pipelines may be only a few miles long or many hundreds of miles.

When mining is finished, the land is restored. Soil is returned to the site and vegetation is replanted. Usually, the mining company is required by federal law to return the land to a state similar to what it was before mining.

# EFFECTS ON THE ENVIRONMENT

Coal mining can have a multitude of adverse effects on the environment, harming plants, animals, and people. It affects the land and water, including rivers and groundwater. Surface mining is particularly harmful because it removes entire habitats. In some instances, mining companies cut down forests or replace agricultural land.

Flooding and landslides can also result from surface coal mining. Trees and plants hold soil in place, and soil soaks up water. When mining rips away the natural landscape, water can collect and flow in ways it normally would not. The Appalachian region has been affected by this destruction.

In July 2022, eastern Kentucky experienced flash floods that killed more than three dozen people. Nicolas Zégre of the University of West Virginia studies the effects of mountaintop removal mining on water and water movement. He notes that global warming and coal mining combined to worsen the environmental effects. Zégre said, "Whether it was the 2016 flood in West Virginia or the recent floods in Kentucky, there's more intense rainfall due to warmer temperatures and then that rainfall was falling on landscapes that have had their forests removed."[3]

Valley fills from surface mining can also be problematic. Rocks and other materials removed during the excavation process

> **Between 2010 and 2020, coal production in the United States declined by nearly 50 percent. But production has been on the rise since 2020.[4]**

are dumped in valleys next to the mining site. These valley fills can hold water for an extended length of time, which can lead to flooding.

Another issue with valley fills is that the material is often contaminated because it contains chemicals and metals used in mining. When the material sits in a valley fill and is exposed to water, the contaminants can wash away and end up in streams. More than 20 percent of streams in central Appalachia have been polluted because of toxic material from mining.[5]

## Centralia Burning

Centralia, Pennsylvania, was once a bustling small town. Coal mining began there in 1850 and defined the town. But in 1962, Centralia changed dramatically. The town dealt with a full garbage dump by setting it on fire. Not long after, the fire reached a coal seam beneath Centralia, and it spread to coal mining tunnels under the town's streets. The fire created hazardous carbon monoxide gas that made mining too dangerous. The town tried multiple times to put the fire out without success. Smoke rose from sinkholes in the ground, and the townspeople began to have health issues. Eventually, the government paid people to leave. The state condemned all the city's buildings in 1992. In 2024, Centralia was still burning.

# FIGHTING COAL MINE EXPANSION IN TURKEY

People in Turkey have also experienced the effects of surface mining. On July 30, 2023, workers in southwestern Turkey finished removing trees in part of Akbelen Forest. The work was for the expansion of a coal mine, and at least 65,000 trees had been cut down.[6] Residents of the nearby village of Ikizköy

Police in Turkey used water cannons and tear gas to break up protests by environmental activists seeking to protect Akbelen Forest.

and beyond were there protesting. Nejla Isik of the Ikizköy Environment Committee said, "They massacred our forest. They destroyed our trees, which we have been protecting for four years, in eight days. As residents of Ikizköy, we do not break our promise until the end. We will fight to the last drop."[7]

The ongoing demonstration had been met with force by the authorities. About 40 people were arrested. Thirty-two percent of Turkey's electricity comes from coal, and the government

## Freya Brown Speaks Out

In September 2019, 16-year-old Australian Freya Brown protested against climate change. She took a stand because she had seen the effects of climate change in her homeland, where friends in rural areas struggled with repeated droughts. Brown knew the neighboring Pacific Islands were struggling with rising sea levels. She said, "It's impacting people disproportionately. We need to be supporting and trying to help those most affected. And realizing some countries have a lot more power and ability to make change."[9] Brown wanted her country to stop new fossil fuel projects. Australia is among the world's biggest coal producers. The country had more than 90 coal mines in operation in 2020.[10]

planned to increase that amount. The governor of Mugla, the province in which Ikizköy is located, said in response to the protest that the deforested area would be "rehabilitated" with the addition of 130,000 young trees.[8]

But the protesters were voicing concern over more than trees. Losing the forest would be detrimental to wildlife, affecting hundreds of species of plants, birds, and mammals. Deforestation could also affect the area's water supply, which would be detrimental to the surrounding farms and to Bodrum, a nearby port city that relies on tourism for income.

Protesters and residents received little support from the government. Instead, an ally of the president accused them of using the environmental cause as a way to protest the government as a whole. In Turkey and around the world, politics and economics often intersect with the environmental impact of coal mining.

# WAYS TO CLEAN UP COAL MINING

Properly restoring mining sites is one way to reduce the harm caused by coal mining. Companies can also use cleaner processes. The organization Empowering Pumps & Equipment works with the energy industry, providing recommendations to make mining more sustainable and less harmful to the environment.

First, it suggests using the latest mining techniques, which are often safer for wildlife and for people than older methods. Empowering Pumps & Equipment also recommends using machinery that is friendlier to the environment. Electric mining equipment is much cleaner than machines powered by fossil fuels because it produces little to no carbon emissions.

The organization also says companies can go beyond the minimum requirements for restoring land after mining is finished. They can take steps to improve the soil, adding organic material to promote future plant regrowth. Coal mining always has an environmental impact, and it will remain a widely used fuel source for the foreseeable future. But steps like these can reduce the harm to the landscapes and ecosystems around mining sites.

> "Global climate change is a momentous issue that calls for a major transition. To create a society that is sustainable in the long term, we need to increase the share of renewable energy—and batteries are playing a key role."[11]
>
> —Epiroc, a company that produces electric mining equipment, 2019

Globally, there are more than 12,000 offshore platforms used to extract oil and natural gas.

CHAPTER 5

# EXTRACTING OIL

Most oil is found in reservoirs deep underground. Often, not all oil in a reservoir can be extracted. That is because doing so may be too costly, difficult, or dangerous. Oil reserves are the accessible parts of a reservoir.

Extracting oil involves drilling a well deep enough to reach the oil. Drilling can be exploratory, developmental, or directional. Exploratory drilling occurs in places where reserves are not known to exist. The cost of exploratory drilling makes it risky, but there is a chance to strike it rich by discovering a reservoir.

Developmental drilling is used where drilling has already proven successful. Directional drilling also occurs in places with known oil reserves. Crews drill down toward the known oil, then drill at an angle in the hopes of finding nearby oil reservoirs.

The location of the oil reservoir determines the type of drilling structure used. Oil rigs or drilling rigs are used on land, and oil platforms drill in water. Drilling in water is considerably more expensive than drilling on land because constructing an oil platform is costly. Oil platforms must be able to withstand harsh conditions in the ocean. Often located far from land, they usually have sleeping and living quarters to accommodate workers.

All drilling relies on a drill bit that spins and pushes into the earth, just as the bit in a handheld drill bores into a piece of wood. Drilling mud supports the process. This substance lubricates the drill bit, keeping it running smoothly. Drilling mud also carries away bits of rock broken by the drill bit, circulating them upward through the well to the surface.

> In 2022, Saudi Aramco was the largest oil company in terms of revenue, earning $590.3 billion.[2]

When a drill reaches a reservoir, the oil may shoot up to the surface with enough pressure to gush several yards into the air. This can be dangerous. Companies use a device called a blowout preventer to keep gushers from happening.

Once a drill reaches oil, pumps pull it from underground. But drilling and pumping extract only a small percentage of the total oil in the reservoir, perhaps as little as 10 percent.[1] Crews can flood wells with water to push more oil to the surface. Today, the most common way to get more out of an oil well is a process known as gas drive. Workers drill deeper than the known oil reservoir, hitting a natural gas reservoir below. The escaping gas pushes out more oil.

## REFINING AND MOVING

Once oil is extracted, it must be refined, or processed. Not all oil is the same. Differences in composition cause significant

Unlike coal miners, oil workers typically do not go underground. But the work still involves large machinery and potential danger.

inconsistencies. Oil classified as light floats on water and is almost entirely made of hydrocarbons.

Heavy oil sinks in water and contains more impurities. Some heavy oils may consist of only half hydrocarbons, with the other half being made up of elements such as copper, iron, nickel nitrogen, and sulfur. The oil may even include sand. The heavier the oil is, the more refining it needs to create usable products. The refining process uses heat to convert oil to kerosene, propane, gasoline, and more. As the oil heats up, its vapors rise and condense at different levels of a tower. For example, gasoline rises higher than kerosene. The various products are collected separately.

The practice of gas flaring releases millions of short tons of greenhouse gases each year.

Pipelines, ships, trains, and trucks transport oil to refineries. After processing, the resulting oil products move to their next destinations using the same methods. Some products are used as they are. Others require further processing before they can be used.

# NEGATIVE EFFECTS ON THE ENVIRONMENT

The processes involved in oil extraction can be harmful to the environment. For example, underwater exploration to locate reserves can hurt or kill fish and other underwater life. And drilling on land usually involves clearing the landscape, which means wiping out ecosystems.

In addition, gas flaring releases chemicals into the environment. Flaring is the burning of the natural gas that escapes the ground during oil drilling. Flares are easy to spot because they are large smokestacks emitting huge flames at drilling sites. The chemicals released include methane and carbon dioxide, which contribute to climate change.

Benzene and naphthalene also result from flaring and can be harmful to humans. Benzene can cause headaches, irregular heartbeat, and shaking. Naphthalene can hurt people's eyes and liver, and it may even cause cancer.

Significant environmental destruction comes from oil spills. Oil spills can occur during pumping when something goes wrong

### Measuring Oil

Oil is measured inconsistently around the world. The United States measures oil in barrels that are approximately 42 gallons (159 L). Rather than measuring by volume, Asia and Europe usually measure oil by weight in metric tons. One metric ton of oil is approximately six to eight barrels of oil.[3] That variance is because not all oil is the same. Oil classified as light is less dense than heavy oil.

## Major Spills

Each year, US waters experience thousands of oil spills. Most are relatively minor, involving the release of a single barrel or less. But many major spills have also occurred. Since the famous 1969 Santa Barbara spill, more than 40 disasters have each involved the release of more than 10,000 barrels, or 420,000 gallons (1.6 million L), of oil.[5] As with the *Deepwater Horizon* rig, many of these spill sites have been in the Gulf of Mexico. Major spills also occurred on the West Coast, the East Coast, and even in a few inland locations.

at a well. They can also occur during transport. Pipelines can leak or break. The ships, trains, and trucks that move oil can have accidents that result in the release of oil.

When oil spills, it poisons the water or ground it covers, affecting wildlife. Simply breathing in oil fumes can be harmful. Oil spills can also result in explosions and fires. A small amount of oil can affect a large area. The National Park Service explains that when oil spills in water, "One drop of oil will cover the area of a two-car garage. One pint [0.5 L] of oil can cover one acre [0.4 ha] of water surface."[4]

Oil spills have short- and long-term effects. Animals may ingest oil by eating something covered in it or by cleaning their bodies after being exposed to it. This can damage the heart or other internal organs, harm the immune system, affect growth, and cause death. Animals that survive may have trouble having offspring.

Seabirds are often the victims of ocean oil spills. Getting oil on their feathers can be deadly, because it can leave the birds unable to fly and damages the waterproofing quality of the feathers.

Oil also removes the insulating quality of sea otters' fur. As a result, birds and sea otters may freeze to death.

# CLEANING UP OIL SPILLS

The long-term effects of an oil spill can be reduced by cleaning up the spilled oil. The cleanup method varies by the location of the spilled oil. Along the shore, workers can rinse oil from the shoreline with hoses, pushing the oil into the water, where it can be removed. Large trucks with vacuums can suck oil from both the shoreline and the water.

Substances called sorbents soak up oil from land. Shovels and front-end loaders are helpful for moving contaminated material. And oil can simply be burned to remove it, although many people are worried about the emissions this method produces.

There are other methods used to clean up spilled oil in the water. Workers can install booms, which are floating barricades that help contain oil to a limited area. Dispersion is a cleanup method where workers add chemicals to the spill that cause the oil to break up. Smaller droplets of oil biodegrade more easily, reducing their effect on the environment.

> " The greatest tragedy will be if we fail to learn from this disaster and to take seriously the need to find alternatives for fossil fuels. But, there are several reasons for hope, starting with human ingenuity and spirit.[6] "
>
> —Sylvia Earle, marine conservationist and ocean explorer, on the 2010 Deepwater Horizon *spill*

Booms provide a physical barrier that prevents an existing oil spill from spreading and getting worse.

Skimming involves boats equipped with devices that float on the water and pull out the oil.

## PROTESTING OIL SPILLS

Many people have protested proposed oil pipelines, arguing that the risks they pose to the environment are too high. In June 2021, approximately 2,000 people protested in and around Park Rapids, Minnesota, against Enbridge Energy's expansion of Line 3, a pipeline that would transport oil through American Indian lands and critical watersheds.[7] Participants picketed, beat drums, and held prayer circles. Some protesters also blocked the road to a construction site for the pipeline. Others climbed over the fence around the site and chained themselves to Enbridge's construction equipment.

Tara Houska, a member of the Couchiching First Nation and an attorney for the band, said of the pipeline expansion, "This is an act of violence on tribal land." Winona LaDuke of Honor the Earth, an organization that supports Indigenous environmental efforts, said, "Taking care of the water is our responsibility, and we take that responsibility seriously. We've been at this fight against Enbridge for seven years already. It's like an invasion."[8]

Ultimately, the police put on riot gear and arrested hundreds of activists. The project continued. On October 17, 2022, the Minnesota Department of Natural Resources said that environmental issues resulting from the construction of Line 3 "have resulted in $11 million in payments, environmental projects, and financial assurances from Enbridge."[9]

### Anti-Protest Laws

In 2020, a West Virginia law called the Critical Infrastructure Protection Act made protesting on oil and gas sites in the state illegal. At the time, two major gas pipelines were planned in West Virginia. People living in the area had been fighting the projects by camping out in trees slated for felling or by locking themselves to construction equipment. The law made these actions illegal and can result in fines of as much as $20,000.[10] West Virginia is not alone with this type of legislation. That year, other states passed similar laws, including Kentucky and South Dakota.

The project had caused multiple aquifer breaches, creating holes in the ground that allow water in underground reservoirs to escape to the surface. Aquifer breaches can cause the earth to sink, which can damage roads and buildings. Such breaches can also lower water levels in lakes, which can hurt the plants and animals that live in these ecosystems. The project had also resulted in 28 spills of drilling mud.[11]

Even as the understanding of the risks of oil extraction and transportation becomes more widespread, oil remains in high demand. Consumption declined dramatically in 2020 as a result of the COVID-19 pandemic, with travel restrictions meaning that gasoline was not needed as much for transportation. But in the following years, oil usage rose again and was projected to soon exceed 2019 levels.

The increase in oil use was driven by people in developing countries using more energy as their standards of living improved. The International Energy Agency reported, "All of this demand growth relative to 2019 is expected to come from emerging and developing economies, underpinned by rising populations and incomes."[12]

## ACTIVIST SPOTLIGHT

# NEMONTE NENQUIMO

Nemonte Nenquimo is a leading voice for Indigenous people in the Amazon rainforest. Born in Ecuador in 1986, she is a member of the Waorani people. The members of this tribe live in the upper Amazon. For several decades, activities such as logging and searching for oil have decimated the Amazon rainforest. Nenquimo fights to save the land of her people and their culture, especially from oil drilling.

With these goals in mind, in 2015, Nenquimo helped create Ceibo Alliance, a nonprofit run by Indigenous people. Among other achievements, in 2019, Nenquimo led a challenge against her government, winning a lawsuit to protect 500,000 acres (202,000 ha) of Amazon land from oil extraction. She declared during the trial, "Our house is not for sale."[13] The case has become a model for other Indigenous groups. Nenquimo has supported Indigenous people in other ways, such as by helping them install solar panels and systems to collect rainwater.

Nenquimo's work has received significant attention. In 2020, she was awarded the Goldman Environmental Prize. This honor "recognizes individuals for sustained and significant efforts to protect and enhance the natural environment, often at great personal risk."[14]

*Time* magazine named Nemonte Nenquimo one of the 100 most influential people of 2020.

In 2022, wells in Texas produced about a quarter of the nation's natural gas.

CHAPTER 6

# EXTRACTING NATURAL GAS

Like oil, most natural gas is in underground reservoirs trapped by rock. Natural gas is often located near oil. And as with oil, it is accessed by drilling into the ground.

Sometimes, to increase the output of a well, a company will use horizontal drilling to access natural gas. This process involves drilling sideways from a known productive spot underground. This way, a new hole does not have to be drilled into Earth's surface.

Extracting natural gas can also involve a process known as acidizing. To get through rock to access natural gas, acidic chemicals may be added to the well. Acidizing increases production of a well and makes it usable for longer.

When natural gas escapes a reservoir, it moves to the surface, where it goes into pipelines that carry it to refineries. As with oil and coal, natural gas contains impurities when it is taken out of the ground. Processing plants remove substances such as carbon dioxide, helium, and sulfur. What remains is almost entirely methane, the main compound that makes up natural gas.

## TRANSPORTING

Pipelines are the most common method of transporting natural gas. The continental United States has an extensive network of natural gas pipelines. A web of more than 210 systems contains more than 300,000 miles (483,000 km) of pipelines and runs through all 48 contiguous states.[1]

Natural gas infrastructure includes much more than just pipelines. Across the United States, more than 1,400 compressor sites keep the natural gas moving through the pipelines. Approximately 400 storage facilities hold natural gas below ground.[2] Thousands of facilities regulate the distribution of natural gas to its final destinations at homes and businesses across the country.

Despite its name, natural gas does not always exist as a gas. Cooling it to approximately −260 degrees Fahrenheit (−162°C) changes it to a liquid, and that liquid is about 600 times denser than the gaseous form of natural gas.[3] The fuel is turned into

### A Cleaner Fossil Fuel?

When it comes to burning fossil fuels, natural gas is cleaner than oil and coal. When burned, natural gas releases 30 percent less carbon dioxide than oil and 45 percent less than coal.[4] Carbon dioxide is the biggest contributor to climate change. Natural gas also emits less mercury, nitrogen oxide, and sulfur dioxide than oil and coal. But natural gas is also mostly methane, the second-largest contributor to climate change, and leaks during production and transport make up a significant portion of overall methane emissions. Methane traps more heat than carbon dioxide does. However, methane lasts seven to 12 years in the atmosphere, and carbon dioxide can last for hundreds of years.[5]

A complex network of ships, tanks, and pipelines is used to store and transport natural gas.

liquid form for transport and storage in locations that lack pipelines. Specially designed tanker trucks carry the liquid natural gas to its destination.

## ENVIRONMENTAL EFFECTS

Like oil drilling, drilling for natural gas has negative effects on the environment. Before drilling, the ground is cleared, eradicating vegetation and wildlife. The drilling itself creates air and noise pollution that can negatively affect wildlife and locals. Drilling can also pollute water sources, and it creates massive amounts of contaminated water. Additionally, the engines that power drilling equipment and the compressors that move natural gas in pipelines emit exhaust and are loud.

Usually, an energy company will clean up a site after drilling for natural gas. That includes removing equipment and returning the site as close to its original appearance as possible. But this work is not always done.

Pipeline leaks are a major environmental concern with natural gas drilling and transport. Leaks release methane into the air, contributing to greenhouse gas emissions. But leaks are a problem for another reason. Natural gas is highly flammable. That means a leak could result in an explosion. And the gas itself is also harmful to human health.

The United States has experienced some extremely dangerous gas leak incidents. The largest US gas leak occurred in 2015 at a natural gas storage site in California's Aliso Canyon, located near Los Angeles. The leak lasted for a few months and released almost 100,000 short tons (91,000 metric tons) of methane and other chemicals into the air, which left numerous residents ill. Thousands of people had to leave their homes.[6]

In 2021, Southern California Gas Company (SoCalGas), who owns the storage site, and its owner, Sempra, agreed to pay as

> **PHMSA**
> The Pipeline and Hazardous Materials Safety Administration (PHMSA) is part of the US Department of Transportation. PHMSA creates and enforces regulations for transporting natural gas and other hazardous substances, ensuring these systems are safe for both people and the environment. PHMSA also works with emergency personnel and the general public, helping people prepare in case an incident such as a gas leak were to occur.

much as $1.8 billion to residents and businesses affected by the leak. This was in response to 35,000 lawsuits that were filed. The head of SoCalGas, Scott Drury, said about the settlement, "These agreements are an important milestone that will help the community and our company work toward putting this difficult chapter behind us."[7]

In the United States, utility companies are required to report natural gas incidents that lead to hospitalization, death, or property damage costing more than $122,000. Between 2010 to 2022, more than 2,700 such incidents occurred across the nation. And 362 of them resulted in explosions. The incidents led to almost 700 injuries and more than 140 deaths.[8]

Leaks can occur for various reasons. A metal pipeline may rust too much and deteriorate. A pipeline component may be loose or damaged. Another cause may be digging. Someone excavating may inadvertently hit a pipeline with their equipment.

Because leaked natural gas escapes into the atmosphere, no cleanup of the ground is needed, as there would be with

### Smelly for Safety

Natural gas is odorless, so a person could not smell it if a leak occurred. To combat this issue, energy companies add a substance called mercaptan to natural gas to make it smell like rotten eggs, an odor that stands out. This is to help in case of residential leaks. Exposure to a leak can cause dizziness, headache, nausea, and more. When someone suspects a gas leak, they should evacuate the area immediately and call 911.

an oil leak. To prevent continued leakage, equipment must be repaired or replaced. In the results of a study regarding fixing natural gas leaks, an environmental organization called Clean Air Task Force noted that repairing leaks promptly is also in a company's best financial interest. It said, "Because fixing leaks saves gas that would otherwise be wasted, it allows companies

to sell more gas. Once the company identifies the leaks, repairing almost every leak pays for itself."[9]

## TAKING A STAND IN SPRINGFIELD

In 2021, protesters gathered outside city hall in Springfield, Massachusetts. The protesters were there to voice their

In 2019, a natural gas pipeline in San Francisco, California, exploded. It caused a significant leak and a severe fire.

In 2016, people from Cummington, Massachusetts, protested to stop a natural gas pipeline from being constructed in the town.

concerns about a proposed five-mile (8 km) pipeline project by Eversource Energy. They described it as "unnecessary, unhealthy, and dangerous."[10]

Protesters were concerned for multiple reasons. One was that state legislators had vowed to decrease the use of fossil fuels in Massachusetts, and the project did not align with that policy. As protester Mireille Bejjani explained, "This project is a test of our state administration. Are they going to rise to the challenge and really center environmental justice and frontline communities in their decision making?"[11]

Another reason was personal for some, including Yvette Hernandez. She was concerned about the possibility of explosions. Members of her family lived in Lawrence, Massachusetts, when natural gas explosions happened there in 2018. "This project that is being proposed to go through our South End community is subjecting our families to an unneeded very very risky project," Hernandez shared.[12]

The demonstration was one of several elements of the protest against the pipeline. Residents, environmental groups, and others planned to place signs in their yards, create a petition, and write letters to legislators. In July 2023, the project was officially halted when Rebecca Tepper, the state's energy and environmental affairs secretary, called for more research by Eversource. She said the company would need to perform "a deeper analysis about how the project would affect the state's climate goals and impact local communities."[13] Eversource had to submit a report that would be subject to review and input by the community and the state.

## REDUCING LEAKS

Gas companies have multiple options for reducing natural gas leaks. The Environmental Defense Fund (EDF), a nonprofit environmental organization, notes several things energy companies can do to reduce natural gas leaks. One of those is improving the monitoring of pipelines.

The EDF is "working with scientists, utilities and technology providers to validate new mobile monitoring equipment and develop new scientific methods to translate the data gathered into actionable information."[14] This includes collecting data on leak locations and sizes. Gas companies can use this data to improve their pipelines and save money, and the data can also help politicians and everyday citizens understand how significant natural gas leaks are.

The EDF has sought more accountability for natural gas leaks. It wants utility companies and state agencies to re-examine their guidelines for repairing leaks, set specific goals

> " I don't think people are aware that it is such a widespread problem, where there are those constant, continuous leaks in our system, in the pipelines that are bringing gas to our homes. They pose this risk that they could light or explode, really at any time.[15] "
>
> —Matt Casale, director of environment campaigns, US Public Interest Research Group, July 2022

Improving the inspection and maintenance of pipelines can reduce the risk of natural gas leaks.

to reduce the number of leaks, and respond more quickly when leaks are detected. On a policy level, the organization has sought tougher laws and regulations on methane emissions.

Stricter rules would incentivize the industry to improve not only the process of repairing leaks but also the process of extracting natural gas. Natural gas companies have considerable power to improve the energy extraction

In 2022, approximately 60 percent of US homes had natural gas connections.[16]

industry's impact on the environment. Focusing on safe, well-maintained pipelines can help both human health and the natural landscapes around pipelines.

Fracking is an effective method of increasing oil and gas production, but its environmental impact has made it a controversial practice.

CHAPTER 7

# FRACKING

While drilling is common for extracting oil and natural gas from deep in the earth, it is not the only method for doing so. Energy companies also use a process called hydraulic fracturing, or fracking. The method has proven productive in terms of accessing these fossil fuels, especially in the United States, where it has boosted production and lowered the need to buy oil and natural gas from other countries. However, it also presents several risks to the environment.

## WHAT IS FRACKING?

Fracking works by shooting a mixture of water, sand, and chemicals at high power into underground rock formations that have fossil fuels. The pressure of the fluid is great enough to fracture, or crack open, the rock. This allows the oil and natural gas to escape and be collected.

Fracking is not new, but two advances in this process of energy extraction led to a boom in the early 2000s. One improvement was using fracking with horizontal drilling.

Fracking starts with drilling a well down into the earth. When the well gets close to the fossil fuel reserves, workers start drilling horizontally. Next, steel pipes go into the well, followed by cement that fills space between the pipes and the rock. The pipes have holes for the fracking fluid to shoot through.

The other change was in the mix of the fracking fluid, which is also called slickwater. Slickwater is almost entirely water, as much as 97 percent.[1] The sand serves as a proppant, a solid material that fills cracks formed by fracking and keeps them open so the oil or natural gas can escape. Often, the sand is a material known as frac sand, which is made of a type of quartz that does not crush easily. Fracking activity at one well can take thousands of short tons of frac sand.

Slickwater contains chemicals, too. The types and amounts of chemicals in the fluid vary by the type of rock being fractured and other factors. For instance, acids break down rock, and some chemicals help keep the steel pipes in the well from degrading.

### Williston, North Dakota

In 2009, the town of Williston, North Dakota, saw a fracking boom. Williston is located on reserves of oil and natural gas. Energy companies flocked to the town, and people soon followed to get work. Williston's population jumped from 12,000 people to more than 30,000 in a few years. But little more than a decade later, Williston went from boom to bust. That is because the cost of oil dropped dramatically in 2014, and the number of active wells dropped from 195 to 64.[2]

# EFFECTS ON THE ENVIRONMENT

Fracking affects land, air, and water. Because fracking involves drilling, the land where a well is drilled is cleared, which removes vegetation. This deforestation can be devastating to wildlife. In addition, fracking uses tremendous amounts of water, sometimes more than one million gallons (3.8 million L) for one well.[3] The EPA reports that fracking uses billions of gallons of water each year in the United States. That leaves less water for people to drink or for farmers to grow crops.

After it is shot into the rock, fracking fluid is collected in tanks or pits aboveground or in wells underground. Leaks and spills of this substance can affect land and water. The wastewater from fracking contains high amounts of salt and can make soil less able to grow vegetation. And the chemicals in the wastewater make it harmful to humans.

## So Much Water

EOG Resources is one of the biggest fracking companies in the United States. Since 2011, EOG has used more than 73 billion gallons (276 billion L) of water for fracking. The company BP has used more than nine billion gallons (34 billion L). Fracking companies are using increasing amounts of water. As a result, in addition to searching for oil and natural gas, they are digging deep for water, especially in Texas, which regularly has droughts. BP has more than 130 water wells there. Even when Texas residents have faced water restrictions, fossil fuel companies have been allowed to use water. According to a 2023 article in the *New York Times*, "Nationwide, fracking has used up nearly 1.5 trillion gallons [5.7 trillion L] of water since 2011. That's how much tap water the entire state of Texas uses in a year."[4]

In the United States, more than one million wells have been created using fracking.

Reports to the EPA revealed that energy companies use more than 1,000 different chemicals in their fracking fluids.[5] Ethylene glycol, methanol, and propargyl alcohol are often found in slickwater and are known to be dangerous for humans. In addition, wastewater can contain oil because it has mixed with the fossil fuel during the fracking process. Leaked wastewater can get into drinking water, making it unsafe.

Another negative effect of fracking is earthquakes. When a fracking project is done, a common practice is to shoot the contaminated water into wells deep in the earth. The resulting underground pressure can be high enough to trigger earthquakes. This is especially true in areas with numerous wells.

For example, West Texas has a history of fossil fuel production. When fracking increased in the region, so did the number of earthquakes with a magnitude of 3.0 or greater. In 2021, the area experienced 209 of these earthquakes, which was more than eight times as many as in 2017. In addition, earthquakes in West Texas have become stronger. Between 2017 and 2021, the number of earthquakes with a magnitude of 4.0 or greater jumped from zero to 15. An earthquake with a magnitude of 4.0 is 32 times stronger than a 3.0 magnitude earthquake.[6]

> The United States produces the greatest amount of frac sand in the world. Between 2005 and 2015, the number of sand mines in Minnesota and Wisconsin doubled.[8]

Christina Bock lives in West Texas, and earthquakes have damaged her property, causing her walls to crack and her deck to detach from her house. Bock described her experience to the *Texas Tribune* in 2022. "In the hardest ones we've experienced, there is a bunch of shaking, and the pictures shook off the walls," she said. "You'll hear a loud bang. If you're inside, you assume it's a car wreck or that something exploded outside. The scary thing is that they are happening pretty much daily at this point."[7]

Fracking affects the air by releasing methane. Leaks during the production, storage, and transport of natural gas are responsible for this. A 2019 study found that fracking has played a significant role in the atmosphere's rising methane levels.

# LAWS AND REGULATIONS AFFECTING FRACKING

Fracking companies do not have to follow some federal laws. For example, the Safe Drinking Water Act does not apply to fracking. Halliburton, an energy company, has been a leader in the fracking industry. In the early 2000s, Dick Cheney was vice president of the United States. His previous job was leading Halliburton as its chief executive officer.

According to Justin Miller in his article "Why It's so Hard to Regulate Fracking," Cheney played a key role in drafting a federal law supporting the fracking industry. Miller wrote, "When Congress passed the Energy Policy Act of 2005, there was a loophole that exempted fracking from safety regulations

Some activists seek to identify and regulate the chemicals used in the fracking process.

stemming from the Safe Drinking Water Act."⁹ Known as the Halliburton Loophole, this exemption permits fracking companies to use chemicals that are otherwise regulated.

Unlike the Safe Drinking Water Act and other federal legislation, some state laws do address fracking. However, states do not usually require fracking companies to disclose the types or quantities of the chemicals used. Companies claim this information is proprietary, meaning they exclusively own it. As a result, for years, the exact chemicals and the amounts used in fracking have been mostly unknown.

The extent of the secrecy extends to health care. Some doctors are not allowed to share fracking chemical information even when it affects their patients. The American Academy of

Family Physicians discusses fracking in an article on its website, noting, "Many of the chemicals used in fracking are protected as proprietary information and may not be publicly disclosed. Some states have even enacted legislation restricting physicians from obtaining or disclosing chemical information even for treatment purposes."[10]

> **Our findings show that excluding fracking from federal regulation under the Safe Drinking Water Act is exposing the public to an array of chemicals that are widely recognized as threats to public health.**[13]
>
> —Vivian R. Underhill and Lourdes Vera, scholars, 2023

But some companies do share some information. Researchers at Northeastern University studied what they could find of such data. Lourdes Vera and Vivian R. Underhill discovered that fossil fuel companies use at least 28 chemicals in fracking that are limited under the Safe Drinking Water Act.[11] Ethylene glycol, an ingredient in antifreeze, was most common. Ethylene glycol is poisonous and can negatively affect the brain, heart, and kidneys. Consuming the substance can be deadly.

Vera and Underhill found that more than 17 million people in the United States live within one mile (1.6 km) of at least one oil or gas well. They also noted that "since 2014, most new oil and gas wells have been fracked."[12] In 2019, Texas had a dramatic increase in the use of benzene, which is known to cause cancer in people.

Another concern that environmentalists have with federal legislation around energy extraction is its age. Many of these laws were passed decades ago and do not take into consideration developments in the fossil fuel industry. That includes the boom in fracking and the resulting need to dispose of billions of gallons of contaminated water.

# WAYS TO CLEAN UP FRACKING

Because fracking involves drilling for oil and natural gas, the methods for cleaning up spilled oil and gas apply, as do post-project efforts such as planting trees at a site. But cleaning up fracking can also involve changes in the process itself. Energy companies can change steps or materials to lessen the negative effects of fracking on the environment.

For example, companies can use recycled water instead of fresh water or not use water at all. Halliburton has equipment that allows any quality of water to be used in fracking. And France's GasFrac uses a gel instead of water.

Additionally, researchers are exploring other ways to

### No Fracking in the Delaware Basin

The Delaware River basin runs through Delaware, New Jersey, New York, and Pennsylvania. The Delaware River Basin Commission (DRBC) is a federal agency charged with overseeing the area, including protecting the river and ensuring the drinking water is safe. In February 2021, after a decade of consideration, the DRBC banned fracking in the basin based on studies showing that fracking contaminates drinking water, groundwater, and surface water such as lakes. The ban includes drilling in areas of New York and Pennsylvania known to have natural gas reserves.

clean up contaminated water. For example, scientists in California and Colorado have studied the use of bacteria to clean polluted water. Cleaning toxic wastewater will prevent the need to store it deep underground.

As with cleaning up water used in fracking, companies can also use equipment that does not rely on oil for power. This will reduce emissions and save on fuel costs. Stopping methane from leaking is also important. In 2015, the EPA addressed this issue with a new regulation. The regulation requires new fracking wells to include equipment in their processes that collect methane rather than let it escape into the atmosphere.

New regulations and practices may also help clean up fracking. Vera and Underhill recommend that Congress end the Halliburton Loophole and create legislation mandating energy companies reveal all the chemicals they use in fracking. The researchers also suggest that fracking information be kept in a single place maintained by the EPA or other government agency. "Fracking could continue for the foreseeable future," the researchers wrote in 2023. "In our view, it's urgent to ensure that it is carried out as safely as possible."[14]

# BANNING FRACKING

Rather than work to improve fracking, the process can be banned altogether. The nonprofit Environment America is a collection of environmental groups representing 30 states. Its website notes that "over 500 communities have taken action to stop fracking."¹⁵ Fracking has been banned in some parts of the United States, though not always permanently. Some cities in Colorado and Texas established fracking bans in the 2010s. But energy companies soon took legal action against the bans, and the rulings in favor of the companies overturned the bans just a few years later. Energy companies have also pushed politicians in Florida and North Carolina to not create laws that ban fracking.

Fracking is controversial internationally as well. In September 2022, UK prime minister Liz Truss decided to lift a national ban on fracking. She said she was seeking to make the country more independent in its energy production at a time when the Russian invasion of Ukraine was disrupting global energy trade.

Protesters quickly rallied against the change. Tina Rothery is active in the Nanas, a group of mostly older women activists who

US Secretary of the Interior Deb Haaland has sought to restrict fracking in certain areas in New Mexico.

had fought to get fracking banned in the United Kingdom. She immediately got to work, returning to the Preston New Road site where she had been previously arrested during other protests.

"It won't just be frontline stuff," Rothery explained. "We will oppose this with legal challenges, planning applications. . . . We will pull out all the stops. . . . We're just going to keep on

People across the world have protested against plans for fracking in their communities.

hammering this until we get the proper ban on fracking."[16] Rothery and the Nanas did not have to protest long. On October 26, 2022, new prime minister Rishi Sunak declared that the fracking ban would remain in place. He said, "We care deeply about passing our children an environment in a better state than we found it ourselves."[17]

Cleaning up the world's energy use is a key factor in reversing and repairing humanity's damage to the environment.

CHAPTER 8

# GET INVOLVED IN SOLUTIONS

In recent decades, people, companies, and governments have become increasingly aware of humans' effect on the environment, particularly as a result of fossil fuel extraction. In response to these environmental changes, many have also begun taking action to make a positive difference. Everyone can take steps to protect the planet from the negative effects of energy extraction.

## CONSERVE ENERGY

One way to limit the consequences of energy extraction is to conserve energy. Using fewer oil-based products and less natural gas and electricity decreases the demand for fossil fuels. Conserving energy can be done multiple ways.

One way is to drive less. Alternatives to driving include biking, walking, or going by public transportation. Carpooling is helpful too. Instead of traveling alone in a car, a person can drive to school or work with coworkers or classmates. Driving an electric car is a good option as well. Any of these choices will help reduce

Taking public transportation such as a subway or bus can help lower greenhouse gas emissions.

the need for fossil fuels. They will also decrease the amount of carbon dioxide emitted. Walking or biking are also great forms of exercise for people.

Actions at home can also conserve energy. An obvious one is to simply turn off lights and appliances when not in use. This includes televisions and computers. People can set thermostats

for furnaces and water heaters at lower temperatures to use less fuel.

Regarding temperature and saving energy, furnaces and air conditioners will use less energy when a home is properly insulated. In addition, keeping air inside saves energy. Warm and cool air can escape through spaces around windows and doors.

> **We understand today that humanity's use of fossil fuels is severely damaging our environment.... Nonetheless, meaningfully changing our ways has been very difficult.**[2]
>
> —Samantha Gross, energy and environmental policy expert, 2020

Caulking and weather stripping can help prevent air from escaping around windows. And adding sweeps to doors to fill in the gap between the door and floor will conserve energy.

Using energy efficient light bulbs and appliances also helps reduce energy consumption. LED light bulbs are great energy savers, using as much as 85 percent less power than an incandescent bulb. And using appliances with an Energy Star label can save as much as 40 percent more energy than other appliances.[1]

# USE RENEWABLE ENERGY SOURCES

An important part of decreasing reliance on fossil fuels is using renewable energy sources. Transitioning to solar power, wind power, and other renewable energy sources will reduce reliance on fossil fuels and lower the demand for them. This, in turn, will reduce the environmental effects of fossil fuel extraction.

Renewable energy use is on the rise across the globe. Many countries have been transitioning from fossil fuels to renewable energy sources, and the United States has begun to do the same. From city buses and delivery vans to public buildings, renewable energy is providing electricity in numerous US cities. A 2023

*New York Times* article noted, "Globally, change is happening at a pace that is surprising even the experts who track it closely." The authors wrote:

> Wind and solar power are breaking records, and renewables are now expected to overtake coal by 2025 as the world's largest source of electricity. Automakers have made electric vehicles central to their business strategies and are openly talking about an expiration date on the internal combustion engine. Heating, cooling, cooking, and some manufacturing are going electric.[3]

The use of home solar panels is on the rise in the United States. A California law requires solar panels on most new homes constructed in 2020 or later.

Almost a quarter of US electricity in 2023 came from renewable sources, which was 10 percent more than in 2013.[4] Everyday consumers are an important part of making this transition happen. For example, purchasing electric cars transitions buyers from gasoline to electricity as an energy source for their vehicles. Furthermore, the purchases show automakers the growing demand for these products and encourage these companies to continue focusing on electric vehicles rather than those powered by fossil fuels.

Another way consumers can transition to renewable energy is by installing solar panels. Americans have been doing so with greater frequency. From 2013 to 2023, solar energy grew 24 percent in the United States. More than three million homes have solar panels. And experts predict that about 15 percent of US houses will have solar panels by 2030.[5]

Wind energy as an alternative energy source is also growing. This renewable resource supplies 10 percent of electricity in the United States, and the figure is increasing.[6] In 2022, wind ranked fourth on the list of all energy sources used in

## Renewable Energy Rising

While fossil fuels continue to be the dominant sources of power worldwide, renewable energy sources are growing in use. In 2022, nonrenewable sources provided 85.6 percent of electricity, and renewable energy provided 14.4 percent. Coal provided 35.4 percent of power worldwide, followed by natural gas at 22.7 percent. Oil provided 2.5 percent. Solar power provided 4.5 percent of electricity, and wind power provided 7.2 percent.[7]

the United States and was the most used renewable energy.[8] According to the American Clean Power Association, more than 70,000 wind turbines could produce enough energy to power 46 million households.[9]

Energy companies own most wind turbines, but individuals have them as well. Before investing in a turbine, people should figure out if their location gets enough wind to make installing a turbine practical. Knowing if the city or country allows turbines is also important.

# BE AN ACTIVIST

Activism is another way to support the environment. Activism can take a variety of forms. One is to use social media to share information about fossil fuels. Topics could include information about the negative effects of energy extraction, including the results of mountaintop removal mining and the dangers of oil spills and natural gas leaks. Providing verified statistics, such as the frequency of these events, can make the scope of the issue clearer to others.

Organizing an event to protest fossil fuels is another option. Activists may take a stand against the expansion of a pipeline or funding of the fossil fuel industry, or they may promote the use of renewable energy sources. Petitions are another way to be an activist. They involve collecting names and signatures of people supporting a cause, such as stopping fossil fuel extraction. Events and petitions are good methods to show collective support for

## ACTIVIST SPOTLIGHT

# JOSH FOX

Josh Fox is a journalist and filmmaker. In 2008, a fossil fuel company offered his family $100,000 to frack on their property. The proposition gave Fox serious doubts about fracking and spurred him to dig into it. He spent the next two years filming what would become *Gasland*, a documentary about fracking. Fox explained, "I discovered an environmental catastrophe like nothing I'd ever seen before. The whole country was getting fracked, and everywhere I went, water was ruined, the air was poisoned, and the land had been scarred, ripped apart, and toxified."[10]

The experience encouraged Fox to become an environmentalist. He received both accolades and admonishment for his work. While his film garnered an Oscar nomination, the fossil fuel industry spoke out against him, and some people in the fossil fuel industry even made death threats. In 2013, Fox released *Gasland Part II*. The film examines more of the long-term effects of fracking, including damage to the environment and harm to the people affected by fracking. It also demonstrates how energy extraction companies respond to criticism using lawsuits and other tactics.

In addition to his documentary work, Josh Fox creates music and theater productions that spotlight social issues.

an issue, and they can be promoted via social media. When planning an event, invite reporters to help spread the word about it.

Following and supporting environmental organizations is another way to be an activist. Several groups exist that endorse ending fossil fuel use or encourage transitioning to renewable energy sources. Among these groups are Earthjustice, the Environmental Defense Fund, Fossil Free, Just Stop Oil, the Natural Resources Defense Council, the Nature Conservancy, the Sierra Club, and the World Wildlife Fund.

Some organizations focus on youth activism. One example is Fridays for Future. Swedish activist Greta Thunberg founded the organization in 2018, when she was 15, to encourage kids worldwide to protest climate change. That includes fighting fossil fuels.

## Environmental Defense Fund

The Environmental Defense Fund (EDF) is a nonprofit organization dedicated to helping the planet and its inhabitants. The EDF began in 1967 when some scientists and lawyers in New York worked to stop the use of the pesticide DDT because it was poisoning birds. Today, the EDF has 1,000 staff members and three million members doing work in more than 30 countries.[11] Projects include supporting the world in changing to clean energy, helping people and nature prepare for and survive climate change, and making air and water cleaner.

# TAKE LEGAL ACTION

Taking legal action is another way to be an environmental activist. Youth in Montana have done just that by taking on fossil fuels.

In August 2023, 16 young people, ages five to 22, went to trial against their state. The plaintiffs sued Montana for "violating their constitutional right to a clean and healthful environment by permitting fossil fuel development without considering its effect on the climate."[12] The two-week trial ended with a ruling in the plaintiffs' favor.

While the judge's decision was in the youth's favor, it did not ensure change. The ruling meant that Montana's lawmakers would have to review the way the state grants permits for fossil fuel extraction and decide whether the permit process needed to change. Still, the ruling brought attention to an important issue. Julia Olson, who represented the plaintiffs in court, issued a statement following the ruling:

*As fires rage in the West, fueled by fossil fuel pollution, today's ruling in Montana is a game-changer that marks a turning point in this generation's efforts to save the planet from the devastating effects of human-caused climate chaos. This is a huge win for Montana, for youth, for democracy, and for our climate. More rulings like this will certainly come.*[13]

## MAKING A CHANGE

People's relationship with fossil fuels and their extraction is complicated. Reliance on fossil fuels is firm, with exploration and excavation continuing. But recent history shows that change is possible. And while efforts by coal, oil, and natural gas companies will have the greatest effects on the extraction processes used

The plaintiffs' victory in the Montana case was an important moment for the legal recognition of climate change issues.

and the environment, other players can make a difference. Governments can pass laws, and regulatory agencies can set regulations. And individuals can take a variety of steps to play their part in fighting the negative effects of fossil fuels.

In 2020, Samantha Gross wrote the article "Why Are Fossil Fuels So Hard to Quit?" for the Brookings Institution, a nonprofit research organization. She stressed that people must understand

People at international conferences such as the United Nations Framework Convention on Climate Change work to create solutions for reducing global usage of fossil fuels.

what fossil fuels are, how they are accessed and processed, and how they are used in order to be able to cope with climate change. Gross said, "Throughout history, humanity's energy use has moved toward more concentrated, convenient, and flexible forms of energy. Understanding the advantages of today's energy sources and the history of past transitions can help us understand how to move toward low-carbon energy sources."[14]

Through understanding and action, change is possible. From the biggest companies and most powerful governments down to communities and individuals, everyone can choose to act in ways that support the planet. Action is needed in order to protect Earth from the extraction and use of fossil fuels.

## Funding the Transition to Renewable Energy

On November 27, 2023, the US Department of Energy announced several projects focused on clean energy. Millions of dollars would be used to help companies transition to renewable energy. One example is in Vernon, Texas, where the funding will be used to help a wind company build turbines. In Weirton, West Virginia, a company plans to manufacture materials essential to clean energy. The government's project also aims to help transition people from working in the fossil fuel industry to the renewable energy industry.

# ESSENTIAL FACTS

## ENERGY EXTRACTION PROBLEMS

- Drilling for oil and natural gas on land requires clearing land, which destroys habitats.

- Mountaintop removal mining destroys landscapes to expose coal for extraction. The process is changing topography and can result in flooding.

- Drilling projects release methane into the air, and methane is the second-leading greenhouse gas contributor.

- Oil extraction can result in spills that destroy countless animals and contaminate land and water.

- The fracking process uses a tremendous amount of water, making that water unavailable to people and animals.

- Fracking also involves injecting wastewater, which is toxic, deep into the earth at high pressures that can cause earthquakes.

## ENERGY EXTRACTION SOLUTIONS

- Proposing steps to help lower the number of methane leaks by natural gas companies and using more sustainable coal mining practices to reduce coal mining's effect on land.

- Enacting fracking laws or banning fracking to prevent the practice from further harming the environment.

- Using renewable energy sources such as solar panels and wind turbines to reduce the need to extract more coal, oil, and natural gas and to lower carbon emissions.

- Taking action against governments to increase regulations on fossil fuel extraction and to enforce the use of cleaner energy sources.

- Getting involved with protests to bring attention to the extraction of fossil fuels in communities and to stop further extraction or new projects.

## TAKING ACTION

- Conserve energy by turning off appliances that aren't in use and using LED light bulbs instead of incandescent bulbs.

- Drive less or get an electric car to lower fossil fuel usage and reduce carbon emissions.

- Organize an event, such as a protest against fossil fuels or for promoting clean energy.

- Support, follow, or join an environmental group.

## QUOTE

"The greatest tragedy will be if we fail to learn from this disaster and to take seriously the need to find alternatives for fossil fuels. But, there are several reasons for hope, starting with human ingenuity and spirit."

—Sylvia Earle, marine conservationist and ocean explorer, on the 2010 Deepwater Horizon *spill*

# GLOSSARY

**aquifer**
An underground rock formation that contains water or allows water to flow through.

**climate change**
A process affecting the planet that is causing global temperatures to rise.

**ecosystem**
A community of interacting organisms and their environment.

**emission**
The production and discharge of something such as smoke, gas, or chemicals into the air.

**fossil fuel**
A natural fuel, such as coal or gas, that contributes to global climate change.

**greenhouse gas**
A gas such as carbon dioxide or methane that absorbs infrared radiation and traps heat in the atmosphere.

**outcrop**
A section of a rock formation at the surface rather than underground.

**plaintiff**
The party that initiates a legal action, such as a lawsuit, against another party.

**pyre**
A pile of burnable material, especially one for burning a body as part of a funeral ceremony.

**reservoir**
An area of oil, usually deep underground.

**seam**
A band, or ribbon, of coal in a rock formation.

**sediment**
Tiny fragments of rock and other particles that settle to the bottom of a body of water.

**settlement**
A legal agreement between two parties to settle a conflict or dispute.

**subsidy**
Money paid, usually by a government, to keep the price of a product or service low.

**turbine**
A machine that uses a fast-moving flow of water, steam, gas, air, or other fluid to produce energy.

**watershed**
A region or area in which water drains into the same body of water.

# ADDITIONAL RESOURCES

## SELECTED BIBLIOGRAPHY

"Actions for a Healthy Planet." *United Nations*, n.d., un.org. Accessed 28 Nov. 2023.

Gross, Samantha. "Why Are Fossil Fuels So Hard to Quit?" *Brookings Institution*, June 2020, brookings.edu. Accessed 28 Nov. 2023.

Thulin, Lila. "How an Oil Spill Inspired the First Earth Day." *Smithsonian Magazine*, 22 Apr. 2019, smithsonianmag.com. Accessed 28 Nov. 2023.

"What Are Fossil Fuels?" *Smithsonian Institution*, n.d., ocean.si.edu. Accessed 28 Nov. 2023.

## FURTHER READINGS

Agrios, Ariana. *Fossil Fuel Industries and the Green Economy*. Greenhaven, 2022.

Butfield, Colin, and Jonnie Hughes. *The Earthshot Prize: A Handbook for Dreamers and Thinkers*. Mobius, 2024.

Mooney, Carla. *Climate Change*. Abdo, 2025.

## ONLINE RESOURCES

To learn more about energy extraction, please visit **abdobooklinks.com** or scan this QR code. These links are routinely monitored and updated to provide the most current information available.

## MORE INFORMATION

For more information on this subject, contact or visit the following organizations:

### Drake Well Museum and Park
202 Museum Ln.
Titusville, PA 16354
drakewell.org
This 240-acre (97 ha) site is where Edwin L. Drake struck oil and started the petroleum industry in the United States. Visitors can tour exhibits, watch films, and explore historic buildings and oil equipment.

### Environmental Defense Fund
257 Park Ave. S.
New York, NY 10010
edf.org
The Environmental Defense Fund offers information about threats to the planet and helps people take action against climate change.

### National Renewable Energy Laboratory
15013 Denver West Pkwy.
Golden, CO 80401
nrel.gov
The National Renewable Energy Laboratory (NREL) employs more than 3,000 people and partners with more than 1,000 organizations in its research on renewable energies, including solar, wind, geothermal, and more.

# SOURCE NOTES

## CHAPTER 1. THE OILY BEACH

1. "Pipeline Information—What Can You Tell Us about the Pipeline Itself?" *Refugio Response Joint Information Center*, 2015, refugioresponse.com. Accessed 28 Feb. 2024.
2. "Refugio Beach Oil Spill." *National Oceanic and Atmospheric Administration*, n.d., darrp.noaa.gov. Accessed 28 Feb. 2024.
3. "Where Are the Pipelines?" *American Petroleum Institute*, n.d., api.org. Accessed 28 Feb. 2024.
4. "Volunteering—How Can I Volunteer to Help?" *Refugio Response Joint Information Center*, 2015, refugioresponse.com. Accessed 28 Feb. 2024.
5. "Refugio Oil Spill Response Evaluation Report: Summary and Recommendations from the Office of Spill Prevention and Response." *California Department of Fish and Wildlife*, May 2018, p. 6, nrm.dfg.ca.gov. Accessed 28 Feb. 2024.
6. "Refugio Oil Spill Response Evaluation Report."
7. Lila Thulin. "How an Oil Spill Inspired the First Earth Day." *Smithsonian Magazine*, 22 Apr. 2019, smithsonianmag.com. Accessed 28 Feb. 2024.
8. Thulin, "Oil Spill Inspired First Earth Day."
9. Thulin, "Oil Spill Inspired First Earth Day."
10. "Refugio Beach Oil Spill."
11. "Refugio Beach Oil Spill."

## CHAPTER 2. THE SCIENCE OF FOSSIL FUELS

1. "Fossil Fuels." *Environmental and Energy Study Institute*, 22 July 2021, eesi.org. Accessed 28 Feb. 2024.
2. Simon Black, Ian Parry, and Nate Vernon. "Fossil Fuel Subsidies Surged to Record $7 Trillion." *International Monetary Fund*, 24 Aug. 2023, imf.org. Accessed 28 Feb. 2024.
3. Hobart M. King. "Coal: What Is Coal and How Does It Form?" *Geology.com*, n.d., geology.com. Accessed 28 Feb. 2024.
4. Joseph P. Riva, Gordon I. Atwater, and Priscilla G. McLeroy. "World Distribution of Oil." *Britannica*, n.d., britannica.com. Accessed 28 Feb. 2024.
5. "Statistical Review of World Energy 2021." *BP*, 2021, bp.com. Accessed 28 Feb. 2024.

## CHAPTER 3. THE HISTORY OF ENERGY EXTRACTION

1. M. Albert Evans and Raja Venkat Ramani. "Coal Mining." *Britannica*, 17 Jan. 2024, britannica.com. Accessed 28 Feb. 2024.
2. Evans and Ramani, "Coal Mining."
3. Andrew Turgeon and Elizabeth Morse. "Petroleum." *National Geographic*, 19 Oct. 2023, education.nationalgeographic.org. Accessed 28 Feb. 2024.
4. Richard Pallardy. "Deepwater Horizon Oil Spill." *Britannica*, n.d., britannica.com. Accessed 28 Feb. 2024.
5. Joseph P. Riva, et al. "Natural Gas." *Britannica*, 26 Feb. 2024, britannica.com. Accessed 28 Feb. 2024.
6. Lisa Friedman. "Ten Years After Deepwater Horizon, U.S. Is Still Vulnerable to Catastrophic Spills." *New York Times*, nytimes.com. Accessed 28 Feb. 2024.
7. Sharon Raissi. "From the Archives: Remembering the New London School Explosion, 86 Years Later." *KETK*, 17 Mar. 2023, ketk.com. Accessed 28 Feb. 2024.

## CHAPTER 4. EXTRACTING COAL

1. "Coal Explained: Mining and Transportation of Coal." *US Energy Information Administration*, 16 Feb. 2023, eia.gov. Accessed 28 Feb. 2024.
2. Raja Venkat Ramani. "Coal Transportation." *Britannica*, n.d., britannica.com. Accessed 28 Feb. 2024.
3. John McCracken. "How Coal Mining Contributed to Deadly Kentucky Floods." *Mother Jones*, 9 Aug. 2022, motherjones.com. Accessed 28 Feb. 2024.
4. "United States Coal Production." *CEIC Data*, n.d., ceicdata.com. Accessed 28 Feb. 2024.
5. McCracken, "Coal Mining Contributed to Deadly Floods."
6. Can Erok and Hamdi First Bayuk. "Turkish Environmentalists Struggle to Save Forest from Coalmine Company." *Balkan Insight*, 3 Aug. 2023, balkaninsight.com. Accessed 28 Feb. 2024.
7. Andrew Wilks. "Locals Vow to Keep Fighting to Save a Forest in Southwest Turkey after the Chainsaws Finish Work." *Associated Press*, 31 July 2023, apnews.com. Accessed 28 Feb. 2024.
8. Wilks, "Locals Vow to Keep Fighting."
9. Somini Sengupta. "Meet 8 Youth Protest Leaders." *New York Times*, 23 Sept. 2019, nytimes.com. Accessed 28 Feb. 2024.
10. "Coal." *Geoscience Australia*, n.d., ga.gov.au. Accessed 28 Feb. 2024.
11. "No Time to Waste." *Epiroc*, 9 May 2019, epiroc.com. Accessed 28 Feb. 2024.

## CHAPTER 5. EXTRACTING OIL

1. Andrew Turgeon and Elizabeth Morse. "Petroleum." *National Geographic*, 19 Oct. 2023, education.nationalgeographic.org. Accessed 28 Feb. 2024.
2. Nathan Reiff. "10 Biggest Oil Companies." *Investopedia*, 13 Dec. 2023, investopedia.com. Accessed 28 Feb. 2024.
3. Turgeon and Morse, "Petroleum."
4. "Effects of Oil Spills." *National Park Service*, 13 June 2017, nps.gov. Accessed 28 Feb. 2024.
5. "Largest Oil Spills Affecting U.S. Waters Since 1969." *National Oceanic and Atmospheric Administration*, 5 Apr. 2017, response.restoration.noaa.gov. Accessed 28 Feb. 2024.
6. Joanna Zelman. "Sylvia Earle Talks Gulf Oil Spill Effects in Exclusive Interview." *HuffPost*, 13 Jan. 2011, huffpost.com. Accessed 28 Feb. 2024.
7. Hiroko Tabuchi, Matt Furber, and Coral Davenport. "Police Make Mass Arrests at Protest against Oil Pipeline." *New York Times*, 7 June 2021, nytimes.com. Accessed 28 Feb. 2024.
8. Tabuchi, Furber, and Davenport, "Police Make Mass Arrests."
9. "Enbridge Line 3 Pipeline Replacement Project." *Minnesota Department of Natural Resources*, n.d., dnr.state.mn.us. Accessed 28 Feb. 2024.
10. Alleen Brown. "A Powerful Petrochemical Lobbying Group Advanced Anti-Protest Legislation in the Midst of the Pandemic." *Intercept*, 7 June 2020, theintercept.com. Accessed 28 Feb. 2024.
11. "Understanding the Line 3 Aquifer Breach and Spills." *Minnesota Environmental Partnership*, 23 Sept. 2021, mepartnership.org. Accessed 28 Feb. 2024.
12. "Oil 2021: Analysis and Forecast to 2026." *International Energy Agency*, Mar. 2021, iea.org. Accessed 28 Feb. 2024.
13. Samantha Newman. "Activist Spotlight: Nemonte Nenquimo." *Seren*, 27 Dec. 2020, seren.bangor.ac.uk. Accessed 28 Feb. 2024.
14. "Overview of the Prize." *Goldman Environmental Prize*, n.d., goldmanprize.org. Accessed 28 Feb. 2024.

# SOURCE NOTES CONTINUED

## CHAPTER 6. EXTRACTING NATURAL GAS

1. Andrew Turgeon and Elizabeth Morse. "Natural Gas." *National Geographic*, 19 Oct. 2023, education.nationalgeographic.org. Accessed 28 Feb. 2024.
2. Turgeon and Morse, "Natural Gas."
3. Turgeon and Morse, "Natural Gas."
4. Hobart M. King. "Uses of Natural Gas." *Geology.com*, n.d., geology.com. Accessed 28 Feb. 2024.
5. "Facts: Methane." *National Aeronautics and Space Administration*, n.d., climate.nasa.gov. Accessed 28 Feb. 2024.
6. Ivan Penn. "SoCal Gas Will Pay Up to $1.8 Billion to Settle Claims from the Nation's Biggest Gas Leak." *New York Times*, 27 Sept. 2021, nytimes.com. Accessed 28 Feb. 2024.
7. Penn, "SoCal Gas Will Pay $1.8 Billion."
8. Joce Sterman. "Silent Threat: Gas Explosions Injured Hundreds, Killed Dozens Nationwide since 2010." *WBTV*, 18 July 2022, wbtv.com. Accessed 28 Feb. 2024.
9. Carbon Limits. "Fixing the Leaks: What Would It Cost to Clean Up Natural Gas Leaks?" *Clean Air Task Force*, cdn.catf.us, p. 2. Accessed 28 Feb. 2024.
10. Paul Tuthill. "Activists Protest Natural Gas Pipeline Project." *WAMC Northeast Public Radio*, 5 Nov. 2021, wamc.org. Accessed 28 Feb. 2024.
11. Tuthill, "Activists Protest Natural Gas Pipeline."
12. Tuthill, "Activists Protest Natural Gas Pipeline."
13. Miriam Wasser. "Mass. Rejects Eversource's Environmental Review of New Gas Pipeline Project in Springfield." *WBUR*, 28 July 2023, wbur.org. Accessed 28 Feb. 2024.
14. "Solutions: Four Steps to Reduce Natural Gas Leaks." *Environmental Defense Fund*, 23 Jan. 2019, edf.org. Accessed 28 Feb. 2024.
15. Sterman, "Silent Threat."
16. "Natural Gas Explained." *US Energy Information Administration*, 28 Apr. 2023, eia.gov. Accessed 28 Feb. 2024.

## CHAPTER 7. FRACKING

1. Melissa Denchak. "Fracking 101." *Natural Resources Defense Council*, 19 Apr. 2019, nrdc.org. Accessed 28 Feb. 2024.
2. Michael Patrick Flanagan Smith. "I Joined the Oil Rush to an American Boomtown. Guess Who Got Rich?" *Guardian*, 6 June 2021, theguardian.com. Accessed 28 Feb. 2024.
3. Melissa Horton. "How Does Fracking Affect the Environment?" *Investopedia*, 17 Apr. 2023, investopedia.com. Accessed 28 Feb. 2024.
4. Hiroko Tabuchi and Blacki Migliozzi. "'Monster Fracks' Are Getting Far Bigger. And Far Thirstier." *New York Times*, 25 Sept. 2023, nytimes.com. Accessed 28 Feb. 2024.
5. Denchak, "Fracking 101."
6. Erin Douglas. "Earthquakes in Texas Doubled in 2021. Scientists Cite Years of Oil Companies Injecting Sludgy Water Underground." *Texas Tribune*, 8 Feb. 2022, texastribune.org. Accessed 28 Feb. 2024.
7. Douglas, "Earthquakes in Texas Doubled in 2021."
8. Denchak, "Fracking 101."
9. Justin Miller. "Why It's So Hard to Regulate Fracking." *American Prospect*, 24 June 2015, prospect.org. Accessed 28 Feb. 2024.

10. "Hydraulic Fracturing (Fracking): Health Effects and Disclosure of Proprietary Information." *American Academy of Family Physicians*, Jan. 2022, aafp.org. Accessed 28 Feb. 2024.

11. Vivian R. Underhill and Lourdes Vera. "Companies that Frack for Oil and Gas Can Keep a Lot of Information Secret—But What They Disclose Shows Widespread Use of Hazardous Chemicals." *Conversation*, 3 Apr. 2023, theconversation.com. Accessed 28 Feb. 2024.

12. Underhill and Vera, "Companies that Frack Can Keep Information Secret."

13. Underhill and Vera, "Companies that Frack Can Keep Information Secret."

14. Underhill and Vera, "Companies that Frack Can Keep Information Secret."

15. "Fighting Fracking: A Toolkit for Activists." *Environment America*, 12 Dec. 2016, environmentamerica.org. Accessed 28 Feb. 2024.

16. Jessica Corbett. "New British PM Blasted for 'Destructive' Decision to Lift Fracking Moratorium." *Common Dreams*, 8 Sept. 2022, commondreams.org. Accessed 28 Feb. 2024.

17. Jessica Elgot and Helena Horton. "Rishi Sunak Will Keep Ban on Fracking in UK, No 10 Confirms." *Guardian*, 26 Oct. 2022, theguardian.com. Accessed 28 Feb. 2024.

## CHAPTER 8. GET INVOLVED IN SOLUTIONS

1. Amanda MacMillan. "Easy Ways to Save Energy at Home." *Natural Resources Defense Council*, 8 Aug. 2023, nrdc.org. Accessed 28 Feb. 2024.

2. Samantha Gross. "Why Are Fossil Fuels So Hard to Quit?" *Brookings Institution*, June 2020, brookings.edu. Accessed 28 Feb. 2024.

3. David Gelles, et al. "The Clean Energy Future Is Arriving Faster than You Think." *New York Times*, 17 Aug. 2023, nytimes.com. Accessed 28 Feb. 2024.

4. Gelles, et al., "Clean Energy Future Is Arriving."

5. Maria Toscano and Michael Dempster. "How Many U.S. Homes Have Solar Panels?" *Consumer Affairs*, 2 Nov. 2023, consumeraffairs.com. Accessed 28 Feb. 2024.

6. "Wind Power Facts." *American Clean Power*, n.d., cleanpower.org. Accessed 28 Feb. 2024.

7. Chris Dickert. "What Electricity Sources Power the World?" *Visual Capitalist*, 10 Sept. 2023, visualcapitalist.com. Accessed 28 Feb. 2024.

8. "Electricity Explained." *US Energy Information Administration*, 30 June 2023, eia.gov. Accessed 28 Feb. 2024.

9. "Wind Power Facts."

10. Natasha Berting. "The Truth Has Changed." *Topia*, 1 June 2022, worldoftopia.com. Accessed 28 Feb. 2024.

11. "About Us." *Environmental Defense Fund*, 2023, edf.org. Accessed 28 Feb. 2024.

12. Amy Beth Hanson and Matthew Brown. "Judge Sides with Young Environmental Activists in First-of-Its-Kind Climate Change Trial in Montana." *PBS*, 14 Aug. 2023, pbs.org. Accessed 28 Feb. 2024.

13. Hanson and Brown, "Judge Sides with Environmental Activists."

14. Gross, "Why Are Fossil Fuels So Hard to Quit?"

# INDEX

air pollution, 20, 40, 63–64, 75, 77, 94
anti-protest laws, 57
Appalachian Mountains, 40, 43–44

benzene, 53, 80
BP, 36, 75
Brown, Freya, 46

carbon dioxide, 53, 61–62, 88
Centralia, Pennsylvania, 44
China, 27, 29–30, 33, 36
Clean Air Task Force, 66
cleaning coal, 40–41
climate change, 20, 22, 46–47, 53, 62, 95, 99
coal mining, 19, 25, 29–33, 39–44, 46–47, 93
    longwall, 32, 39
    room-and-pillar, 39
    shortwall, 39
    surface, 40, 43–44
    thick-seam, 39–40
conserving energy, 87–90

*Deepwater Horizon*, 35–36, 54–55
deforestation, 46, 75
Delaware River Basin Commission (DRBC), 81
Drake, Edwin L., 35
drilling, 13–14, 19, 24–25, 29, 32–33, 39–40, 49–50, 53, 58–59, 61, 63–64, 73–75, 81
    coal, 25, 32, 39–40
    fracking, 73–75, 81
    natural gas, 24, 61, 63–64, 73, 81
    oil, 13–14, 24, 33, 49–50, 53, 58–59, 73, 81

Earth Day, 14
Empowering Pumps & Equipment, 47
England, 31–32, 36
Environmental Defense Fund (EDF), 70, 95
Environmental Protection Agency (EPA), 15, 75–76, 82
EOG Resources, 75
Eversource Energy, 69
*Exxon Valdez*, 35

fossil fuels, 19–23, 25, 27, 29–30, 37, 46–47, 55, 62, 69, 73–77, 80–81, 87–88, 90, 92–99
    regulations, 15, 33, 37, 62, 64, 71, 78–80, 82, 97
    subsidies, 20
Fox, Josh, 94
fracking, 73–85, 94
    earthquakes, 76–77
    fracking fluid, 73–76
    slickwater, 74, 76
    wastewater, 75–76, 82

gas flaring, 53
geologists, 22–25
global warming, 22, 43
Gross, Samantha, 90, 97–99
Gulf of Mexico, 35–36, 54

Halliburton, 78–79, 81–82
Hopi peoples, 30
hydrocarbons, 30, 51

impurities, 40, 51, 61

measuring oil, 53
methane, 53, 61–62, 64, 71, 77, 82

Middle East, 26, 30
Miller, Justin, 78
Missouri, 33
Montana, 95–96
mountaintop removal, 33, 40, 43, 93

Nenquimo, Nemonte, 59
New London, Texas, 37

oil spills, 6, 8, 10–16, 35, 53–55, 81, 93
   cleaning, 6–11, 55–56
   effects on animals, 14, 54–55

peat, 21–22
petrochemicals, 22
Pipeline and Hazardous Materials Safety Administration (PHMSA), 64
pipelines, 6, 14–16, 32–33, 36, 42, 52, 54, 56–57, 61–65, 69–71, 74, 93
   leaks, 6, 37, 54, 62, 64–67, 70–71, 93
   Line 3 pipeline, 56–57
   mercaptan, 65
plankton, 20–21, 27

Refugio State Beach, 5, 10–11, 14–16
renewable energy, 47, 90–93, 95, 99
   funding, 99
   solar, 59, 90–92
   wind, 90–93, 99
reserves, 26–27, 35, 37, 49, 53, 74, 81
   coal, 27
   oil, 26–27, 35, 37, 49, 53, 74
   natural gas, 27, 37, 74, 81

reservoirs, 49–50, 58, 61
Rothery, Tina, 83–85
Russia, 27, 83

Safe Drinking Water Act, 78–80
Santa Barbara oil spill, 12–14, 35, 54
seismic surveys, 23
shaft mines, 32
Southern California Gas Company (SoCalGas), 64–65
Springfield, Massachusetts, 67–69

transporting fossil fuels, 6, 19, 29, 33, 35–37, 39–42, 52, 54, 56, 58, 62–64, 77
   coal, 33, 39–42
   oil, 6, 35, 52, 54, 56, 58
   natural gas, 36–37, 62–64, 77
Turkey protests, 44–46

Underhill, Vivian R., 80, 82

Vera, Lourdes, 80, 82

water contamination, 6, 13–14, 35, 43–44, 46, 54–55, 63, 75–76, 81–82, 94
wells, 33, 35, 50, 74–77, 80, 82
West Virginia, 40, 43, 57, 99
Williston, North Dakota, 74

Zégre, Nicolas, 43

## ABOUT THE AUTHOR

### REBECCA ROWELL

Rebecca Rowell has put her degree in publishing and writing to work as an editor and as an author, working on dozens of books. Recent topics as an author include the brands Gatorade and Nike, and surviving being lost at sea. She lives in Minneapolis, Minnesota.